SAUERKRAUT
AND
ENTERPRISE

SAUERKRAUT

MCCLELLAND AND STEWART LIMITED

TORONTO / MONTREAL

AND ENTERPRISE

BY EDNA STAEBLER

ILLUSTRATED BY VLASTA VAN KAMPEN

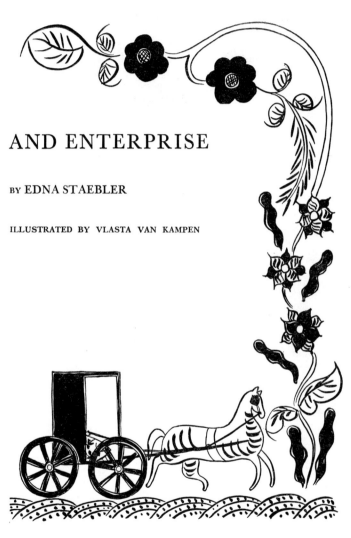

We are indebted to the
University Women's Club of Kitchener-Waterloo
and to Maclean-Hunter Publishing Company
for permission to reprint the material
in this volume.

The Canadian Publishers
McClelland and Stewart Limited
25 Hollinger Road, Toronto 16

Printed and bound in England by
Hazell Watson and Viney Ltd,
Aylesbury, Bucks

CONTENTS

INTRODUCTION

For more than a dozen years now, my family and I have been visiting the Stratford Festival, and only incidentally because we are mad for Shakespeare. The real reason we all go to Stratford is that it gives us an excuse to visit Edna Staebler and eat several bushels of her Mennonite bean salad. Nowhere in the world, not even at the most opulent and fabled *caravanserai*, can any chef hope to approach Mrs. Staebler's bean salad. Even my wife, who is perhaps the world's finest cook, hasn't quite been able to match it.

Edna brings to her writing the same qualities of subtle perfection that she brings to her bean salad. She has a way of picking up speech patterns and atmosphere, sometimes with a single phrase, that any writer must envy. In this little book, already a fabulous best seller in the Kitchener area, she deals with the country and the people she knows best: the Mennonites and Amish who live in the three pioneer

Ontario counties of Perth, Oxford and Waterloo.

I have been over the backroads of these counties myself with Edna as a guide, riding, on one occasion, in an ancient square-roofed buggy, which the Amish call a *Dachwaegle*. There are dozens of tiny red brick villages in this area with names like Conestoga and Heidelburg, each cupped in the hollow of a valley hard by an ancient mill site, each with its steeple or belltower, Bavarian or Swiss, poking up above the trees.

At Hawkesville, I remember, Edna and I found an old harness shop still in operation not far from the spot where John Diefenbaker's father was born. At Heidelburg we came upon a tavern that seemed to leap from the pages of a history book. At St. Jacob's – a little gem of a village (where the bricks are handbaked from local clay and the basements ingeniously constructed of fieldstone rubble) – a blacksmith shop was still plying its trade.

This is Edna Staebler country. She lives in the centre of it – in a gay little cottage on the rim of a lake so tiny that it has mercifully been spared the cacaphony of the power boat. A procession of writers, pretending that they are going to Stratford to soak up culture, manage to find their way to Edna's front door. They come for the bean salad, the conversation and a curious kind of serenity which seems to be the special property of this tiny, fascinating corner of Canada. I think that the reader will find something of that serenity and much of that fascination in the pages that follow. I'm only sorry that it's not possible to attach with every copy a small sample of Edna's bean salad. No words of mine can do it justice.

Pierre Berton

8

THE OLD ORDER
MENNONITES
OF
WATERLOO
COUNTY

NOT LONG ago I stayed for a week with the family of Grossdoddy Martin, in the fieldstone house which his great-grandfather built in the days when the Mennonites came up from Pennsylvania to break new ground in Upper Canada. The house and the family are among the oldest in Ontario – 169 years have passed fruitfully and peacefully over them and the farm their pioneer forefathers cleared from the wilderness in Waterloo County.

The Martins belong to the splinter sect of Old Order Mennonites whose ways often seem strange to outsiders. They shun everything worldly, everything fashionable, but they don't mind a swig of cider. They use electricity and tractors, but will not buy cars or radios. They won't face a camera. They don't have telephones in their homes, or musical instruments. They refuse old age pensions and family allowances. They won't buy insurance or stocks. They won't go to court or to war and Canadian law has been amended to exempt them permanently. They speak Pennsylvania Dutch and have a look of quiet contentment.

The style of their plain, sombre clothes has changed little since 1525. The men wear broad-brimmed black hats with round crowns; their coats, with old-fashioned cut-away backs, are buttoned straight up the front to a neckband, having no collars or lapels. Their faces are cleanshaven; moustaches, being ornamental, are not allowed; the hair of some men and boys is conventionally cut, others look as if a bowl had been placed over the head and the rim used as a cutting guide.

The women's dark print dresses, made from a traditional pattern, have basque waists under a pointed plastron, and long, gathered skirts that almost hide their black cotton stockings. Their uncut, uncurled hair is always covered by an organdie cap tied under the chin, or a helmet-like black satin bonnet. In cold weather they are bundled in shawls. They wear no cosmetics or jewelry – not even wedding rings.

The Old Order Mennonites try to preserve the ways of their forefathers who crossed the Atlantic nearly 300 years ago to escape religious persecution in Switzerland and settled first in Pennsylvania, then, in 1800 came to Canada. Although there are more than 160,000 Mennonites of various sects all the way from Ontario to British Columbia there are only about 2500 members of the Old Order. They cling to their homesteads near Waterloo and Kitchener and their eight similar white clapboard churches are on their own farmlands within a twenty-mile radius.

Like most Old Mennonite farm homes, Grossdoddy Martin's house sprawls. The main house,

Georgian Colonial in style, is broad with a gabled roof, the plastered wall under the porch is painted sky blue. Adjoining is the doddy house, a small addition to which the generations of old folks have retired when their sons took over the farm. Behind the kitchen is the frame summer kitchen; beyond it the wash house, the woodshed, and the privy.

Prosperity smiles on the Martin house from its great painted barn. Beauty surrounds it: gentle hills form its horizons, its fields slope to the maple woods along the curving Conestoga River. On the day I arrived fruit trees beside the house were snowy with blossom and daffodils bordered the neatly fenced lawn.

"You don't want to make fun of us?" The Martins were anxious when I asked if I might live with them for a few days to learn and write about them – though trustful, they were alert. From the beginning they used my Christian name; they were friendly, natural, and disarmingly candid. They answered my questions thoughtfully, generously, and asked me as many in return – only Grossdoddy, listening with a quiet smile, took no part.

I wanted them to speak in their dialect, an unwritten mixture of Swiss-German and English, but they didn't think it would be polite since I couldn't understand all the words. They asked me to correct their English.

"We're shy to talk English in front of strangers because we don't say our letters always right: like for Jesus we say 'Cheesus'. We know it's wrong but we forget. Amongst ourselfs we always talk our own kind of German – it's easier; and if we don't, our own people think we're putting on style."

In their house there was little that was not useful except, in the spare room, two bouquets of paper roses that the parents had given the daughters for Christmas, and calendars that had long outlived their dates. All the walls were whitewashed, the woodwork was painted bright blue. The windows had no curtains, but tins of geraniums bloomed on the sills. There were five bedrooms with pumpkin-yellow floors. The tiny parlor had a huge corner cupboard and wooden chairs set side by side against the pictureless walls. The kitchen was the living-room, the black stove was always warm, and there was comfort in the couch and the rocker in the corner.

"Make the light on once," Bevvy, the mother, directed after supper on the day I arrived, and the family gathered round the big square oilcloth-covered table. David, the father, worked on his income-tax papers; Salome, 16, was absorbed by a romantic novel; Amsey, 7, and Lyddy Ann, 12, smiled at me over their school books; Bevvy placidly turned the pages of the Family Herald; Grossdoddy sat in the shadows near the passage to the doddy house.

"I was glad to quit school and earn money when I was eleven but often now I wish I went longer yet." David frowned at his papers. "If a person went to college his mind would mature in more of a hurry, I guess."

"The teacher wanted Salome to go longer," Bevvy told me. "She finished school already when she was 13, but Mannassah Brubacher's wife needed help chust then, so she went there to work. People hate us for our different ways and if she was in town she would have to act like a turtle for shame or change her Old Mennonite clothes, then she couldn't belong to us no more."

Salome looked up. "I'd like to learn but I wouldn't want to stay from home," she said. "In the city it seems each day is chust like any other day but in the country every day gives something different."

"You can always learn from things you read and people you meet," David's eyes were teasing as they glanced my way. "You think you're going to find out all about us while you're here, but we'll get chust as much from you."

At 9:30 Bevvy led me up an enclosed stair, through a bare corridor to the spare room where I slept surprisingly well on an ancient rope bed with a straw tick and bolster.

Always the first up in the morning, Grossdoddy put on his stay-at-home suit over the long underwear in which he slept – I was told – and went into the parlor of the doddy house where Grossmommy, a black kerchief on her head, lay sleeping on a hospital bed. A young man rose stiffly from a couch.

"She made nothing out all night," he said, putting on his hat. "I see you next week again." He shook the old man's hand, then went out to harness his horse.

He was one of the relatives or neighbours who, in the kindly custom of the Old Order, took turns to come every night from nine o'clock till dawn to relieve the Martin family of some of the care of Grossmommy's lingering illness.

"We always look after our own," Bevvy told me. "And if we don't have enough money for doctors it's paid from the church. We don't take Old Age Pensions or the Family Allowance from the government."

"Why not?"

"If we did we wouldn't feel independent," she said. "You know we got promised religious freedom a long time ago and that our men don't have to fight in a war."

"Would they if our own country was attacked?" I asked.

Bevvy slowly, thoughtfully shook her head. "Jesus said we must turn the other cheek, if everyone did that there would be no wars."

"But everyone in the world doesn't practise Jesus' teaching."

"Then we must be an example," Bevvy smiled. "In the last war our boys helped with the wounded and went in work camps and we bought war bonds." She added hastily, "But we didn't take the interest off them, that would be profiting from war."

When the morning milking was finished, Salome, singing "Throw out the Lifeline," in her clear young voice, drew the full cans to the cooler in a little cart. Topsy, the collie, followed her.

The hens and beeplings fed, Lyddy Ann pointed out a red patch by the river. "Amsey went fishing at five already. Can you see him down there near the willow?"

At the kitchen sink David pumped rain water into the basin to wash his face and arms. Bevvy, by the range, ran plump fingers through the curds that would be made into kochkase (cook cheese).

"Make the door shut, Salome, we won't wait for Amsey." David was hungry, he had been doing barn chores for almost two hours.

Bevvy tucked a wisp of hair under the gray kerchief that had covered her head during the night. "I'll comb myself after breakfast," she said.

Chairs were drawn up to the table, heads bowed silently over iron-stone plates. Grossdoddy reached for coffee cake with his fork. Everyone stabbed a piece and dunked it. Amsey came in, pleased with ten pink-headed chub. Porridge was eaten, the remains sopped up with bread so the plates could be

14

filled with fried potatoes, summer sausage and pickled beans. A bowl of schnitz und gwetcha (boiled dried apple segments and prunes) was passed.

There was talk of the day's work to be done, of things growing, there were questions and answers and there was laughter.

"Dat, you said slang," little Amsey chided his big Mennonite father with the warm brown eyes.

"Did I? Now what bad word did I say?" David pretended alarm.

"You said 'swell'," the child was very serious.

"Och, ain't that awful? I must be more careful or my children won't be brought up decent," David declared. "But ain't 'swell' a bad word that could be used good?"

When we rose the plates looked as clean as when we sat down. Though it was only 7:30 Amsey and Lyddy Ann, eager to play with other children, ran across the fields to school. David went to plow with the tractor, Grossdoddy sat with Grossmommy, Salome sang as she washed the breakfast dishes.

At the little mirror above the kitchen sink Bevvy combed her hair which fell below her waist. "We never cut them," she told me, "and we all do them chust about the same."

Parting her hair in the centre, she wet it to straighten its curl, folded it flat at the sides like the wings of a bird and then wound it into a spiral pinned firmly on the back of her head. As she tied a dainty white organdie bonnet with black ribbons under her chin she said, "It's in the Bible that women should keep their heads covered when they pray and we might pray any time of the day or night." Bevvy never sounds pious, she accepts her rules as she does the planting of seed and the harvest.

Salome, looking through the window above the

sink, exclaimed, "Isn't that pear tree beautiful? I often thought already I'd like to be able to draw it."

"May you draw pictures?" I asked.

"I may but I couldn't," she said.

"We chust mayn't have pictures on our walls or make pictures of ourselfs," Bevvy explained. "It's in the Ten Commandments, you know, about not making a likeness. Our retired bishop is real old and his children in Pennsylvania want him in the worst way to spend the rest of his days with them but he can't because he would have to have his picture taken for a passport and that would set a bad example."

Among the Old Mennonites example is a powerful force, I learned from the Martins. Young people emulate those who are older, the preachers urge adherence to the ways of their ancestors. If these humble people are permitted any pride, it is in their traditions. Their forefathers braved perils and hardships for their faith, clung to their beliefs and died for them.

The Mennonite creed arose when the establishment of a state church in Switzerland was opposed in 1525 by a group of ex-monks and scholars who wanted a religious order that was free of compulsion. The new sect spread rapidly over North Switzerland; it taught only love, faith, forbearance, and adult baptism but its followers were exiled, tortured, or burned at the stake. Believing that evil would be overcome by goodness, they would not defend themselves against attack, and thousands of martyrs died without offering resistance.

In 1538 Menno Simons, a former Roman Catholic priest who had become a convert, reorganized and consolidated their congregations – which became known by his name. Services were held secretly in houses and barns; when educated leaders were im-

prisoned or murdered, simple farmers chosen by lot became preachers and bishops. The humble Mennonites, evicted from one place, would patiently begin again in another till they ranged throughout central Europe. Wherever they settled the land blossomed under their care.

Persecution continued for over two hundred years. From 1683 on, thousands of Mennonites accepted the invitation of William Penn – whose Quaker faith was similar to theirs – to come to America where Britain promised them freedom from military service and the right to worship as they pleased.

Because they wanted to keep the security of British citizenship after the American Revolution, and because land was less expensive in Upper Canada than in Pennsylvania, hundreds of Mennonites brought their families in Conestoga wagons on the seven weeks' journey across swamps, mountains, and the terrifying Niagara. Some stayed near the Canadian frontier but most pushed on to Waterloo County where they became the first white settlers in the interior of the province.

"And from them came all the different kinds of Mennonites around here," David told me.

"Except the Mennonites that came over from Russia," Bevvy corrected.

"Yah, that's right. We don't know much about any but our own. The others mostly all have churches in the towns and they don't dress or act like us Old Mennonites." In this way David dismissed the majority of Mennonite sects.

The first break from the pioneer church in Waterloo County was made in 1869 when, with bell, book, and candle, a group was ceremoniously evicted because it wanted evangelism. The desire for English services, camp meetings, Sunday schools, young people's societies, higher education, the free use of invention, of modern but modest dress, resulted in further divisions. Quite separate but similar were the 15,000 Mennonites who came from Russia in 1874 and settled in Manitoba and Saskatchewan and the thousands who were forced from their homes by the Bolsheviks in the 1920's and found refuge in Ontario and western Canada.

"In Kitchener there is a Mennonite High School, and in Waterloo an Old People's home and a college at Waterloo University," Bevvy told me. "And they have a Mennonite Central Committee where all the kinds of Mennonites go together and sew and send food and clothes and implements to Mennonites in other parts of the world to give to people in need, no matter who they are. I think that's real nice but our old folks don't want us to work in town so we have sewing bees in our own homes and send the Committee what we make." Because it might seem boastful, Bevvy went on reluctantly. "We give them food and money too but we mostly just care for our neighbours and our own: like if a man's barn burns down we build him a new one, if his cows die we give him some, or we help with his work if he's sick. That's the Golden Rule," she said simply.

"Why aren't there more Old Order Mennonites?" I asked.

Bevvy blushed. "In Canada there's only us around here."

"There's some in Pennsylvania and Ohio," David said, "only they're a little different from us yet, but we visit back and forth and are related with each other."

"We can marry back and forth too," Bevvy added, "but it's chenerally only the leftovers that do; most

19

Old Mennonites get partners at home where their parents can buy them a farm."

"We like to stay all together like," David explained. "It makes it easier for us to keep our rules if we aren't mixed up with other people."

"Do you think the rest of us are so bad?" I asked.

"Ach no," Bevvy was embarrassed. "We think there's good and bad the same as with us, we chust have different ways."

"Like the Newborns," David said, "they broke off from us because they thought we were going too fast by having the electric and tractors; they wanted to be more backward yet. And the Markham Mennonites wanted cars and telephones so they got out, but they still use our churches every other Sunday and they paint their cars black with no chrome."

One day the roadside post box had a packet in it for Salome. "It's the books we sent for with the box tops." She opened it excitedly. One book was a novel, the other a collection of old songs from which she started singing "My darling Nellie Gray." If I had told her that her voice is beautiful she would have blushed and had no ambitious or vain thought of performing on radio, television, or in Hollywood – though she has eagerness, imagination, wit, a gay red mouth, merry eyes and the roundest of elbows. When a strand of her soft brown hair escapes its severity her mother reproves her, but Salome laughingly says, "It looks nicest when it's shtruvelich (tousled)."

"Here comes Uncle Isaiah." Lyddy Ann had started reading Salome's novel the moment she came home from school but she reported every movement on the road. An old man with a strong stern face came into the kitchen and shook hands all around.

"How is Auntie Katie?" Bevvy asked him.

"She ain't goot. She's got the high blood pressure yet and the doctor says she must lose some fat but she can't – it's natural. Her mother and father together weighed 500 pounds." The old man shook his head despairingly, then settled in a corner to chat with Grossdoddy.

While we peeled potatoes for supper Bevvy said to me, "You haf such a nice apron."

"I'll let you have the pattern for it."

She grinned. "No thanks, we couldn't have one so fancy. Our clothes are supposed to be all alike and plain so we won't think about how we look. They protect us from temptation too, we couldn't go to wicked places like picture shows without being noticed."

"Leave me show her how we dress in winter." Salome ran upstairs; in a few minutes she was back, shaped like an enormous black beehive, only her delicate nose and sparkling eyes revealed the lovely girl.

"Salome, I wouldn't know you if we met on the street," I exclaimed.

"You would," she laughed, "I'd yell at you."

A wool crepe veil was folded over her forehead and pinned around the satin bonnet, a thick fringed shawl fastened with a blanket pin covered a loose black coat, a smaller shawl muffled her chin.

"It's cold in an open cutter," she explained as she took off the layers of clothes. "See, I fold my shawl straight – if I was married I'd have a point down the back." She handed me her black satin bonnet; it was stiff and heavy as a steel helmet and a little bit faded. "That I had since I finished school already."

"She'll have to take good care of it till she's twenty-

21

one, then we'll buy her a whole new outfit and have her bonnet made over," Bevvy told me while Salome returned her things to the closet.

"Is that when she'll be married?"

"Not necessary, but she might be if she's found a partner she likes. Every Sunday evening the young folks go together to someone's house for a 'singing'; they learn our hymns that way and play games and Salome says some of them dance – but they're not supposed to. If a boy and girl like each other he might drive her home in his buggy."

I faltered over my next question: "Do they bundle?"

"Bundle? What's that?" Bevvy's innocence was honest; I couldn't pursue the subject.

"Does she go out with different boys?" I asked.

"Och no, she sticks to the one she chooses at the beginning, usually. She could fire him at the end of a year or two and go with another but never more than two or she'd have a bad name and for the boys it's the same – no girl would want to go with a boy that would run from one to another. It's not like in the city where young people go out with strangers; we know the parents and grandparents of everybody from way back and we can pretty well tell if a marriage will be all right. We mayn't have divorces. Only one Old Mennonite married man we know ever went with another woman, and of course now he's out of the church."

After supper the children were in a gay mood. They cleaned the fish Amsey had caught, they patted the cats, Lyddy Ann picked violets, Salome played her mouth organ (the only musical instrument allowed), they pranced around the pansy bed, Lyddy Ann held sticks for Topsy to jump at, Salome sang a song. We smelled the honeysuckle and the daffodils; when darkness came we looked at the stars.

"I often wondered already how the street lights look when they're on in Kitchener," Salome said wistfully.

"Do you never go to town?" I asked. Kitchener was only eight miles away.

"Oh yes, to the dentist."

"But we have always to be home in time for the milking," Lyddy Ann lamented.

Amsey was looking at the North Star. "I would like once to see a ship," he declared.

"I too," said Lyddy Ann. "I would like to travel round the world."

"I would go with you," the little boy said, "and if we came to some cannibals they would eat me last because I am the skinniest."

At nine o'clock Bevvy called, "Come in now, children, and wash your feet before you go in bed."

On Sunday morning Grossdoddy drove Salome and me to church; he sat on one of each of our knees while we sat on the narrow seat of his buggy.

Martin's Meeting House on the highway north of Waterloo is more than a hundred years old; its painted clapboards gleam white. A wire fence surrounds its yard, kept neat by a munching cow, and the cemetery beside it where rows and rows of plain white slabs mark the grassy, flowerless graves. There are no family plots, here Nathaniel Lichty, Josiah Ernst, Susannah Eby, Israel Weber, Veronica Erb, Rebecca Shantz – and the still-born infants of David and Bevvy Martin – lie side by side.

Open buggies, two-seaters and box-like dachwaegles (top buggies) came in a steady stream as the black-clad people gathered to worship. Horses pranced up to the cement stoop along one side of the building, women and little girls in shawls and bonnets

23

alighted; grandmothers went through a door near the front, mothers and children near the centre, young girls hurried to the back. Men and boys drove to the hitching chains then entered the church on the farther end. In a crowded cloakroom on the women's side, shawls hung on wooden pegs, black bonnets lay on shelves; on the heads of the rosy-cheeked chattering girls were caps of white organdie with pale coloured ribbons tied under their chins – the style of their hair and their print cotton dresses had no variation.

Light flooded the church from small-paned windows, walls were whitewashed, scrubbed pine floors and benches were worn smooth and shiny. Women sat on one side, men on the other, on benches that were half the length of the church, each bench a step higher than the one in front of it. In the aisle between them were two stoves with long smoke-stacks. Suspended from the ceiling above each bench on the men's side were wooden bars with wooden pegs for the men's broad-brimmed hats.

A long desk-like lectern in the centre front of the church had an open space before it to be used for baptism and feet-washing ceremonies. Behind the lectern five men sat side by side; a sixth man approached, kissed and shook hands with the others, then took his place among them.

"That's our preacher," Salome whispered to me. "The others are preachers too and our bishop."

Chosen for life by lot from slips of paper drawn from a Bible, the Old Order Mennonite preacher, Salome told me, is also a farmer. He receives no pay, prepares no sermons, his spontaneous word is believed to be inspired. And he has authority. If a church member buys what he is not supposed to,

24

marries outside the Old Order, gets drunk too often, or does worldly things, the preacher will speak to him privately. If the vanity or sin is not repented, if it is irremissible, the erring one is denounced before the congregation. Though cast out of the church he is not treated unkindly and, if contrite, may return.

Salome opened a hymn book printed in German script. Led by a man's voice, the congregation sat while it droned each syllable; the bishop preached for half an hour. The congregation, turning to face their seats, knelt for silent prayer, their backs to the front of the church. "To live honestly and at peace with all men" was the text of the preacher's hour-long sermon in Pennsylvania Dutch.

Throughout the service the older men and women sat very still but in the long benches in front there was constant movement of babies and tiny children being hushed or taken to the cloakroom by mothers with bulging satchels. Two rows of lively little girls, their braids tied with string or a bit of shoelace, couldn't restrain a few giggles. The young girls who sat high at the back of the church turned solemn eyes towards the preacher or stole glances at the young men on the high benches at the other side of the room.

During the last hymn the little ones filed into the cloakroom; babies in bright print or lustre dresses, black stockings and colorful bootees, were bundled up in dark shawls. The service over, women and children clustered on the cement stoop to chat till their men drove up smartly to pick them up in their buggies or two-seated wagons.

Salome blushingly told me she was invited out for the day.

"Sunday is our visiting day," Bevvy explained. "Sometimes we have twenty people drop in for a meal."

"And don't you know they're coming?" I asked.

"Not always, they chust come after church. When Menno Horsts moved to the farm over there behind those maples they had fifty-six the first Sunday," She smiled. "Everyone was inquisitif to see their new house."

"How do you feed them?"

"Ach, that don't bother us, everybody helps. There's always lots in the cellar or the garden, and every Friday we bake cakes and buns and nine or ten pies. If somebody comes they're all eaten at one time and if not we haf them the rest of the week."

During the next three days the Martins answered many more of my questions.

"The preachers tell us to vote if we need a new bridge or something like that, but we don't know enough about politics to vote for the country. Artificial insemination of our cattle gives us better stock. With electricity we can do more work. Salome can run the tractor. Telephones we may have in the barn for business – if we sell fresh meat or the like of that – but not in our houses for pleasure.

"We wouldn't want our children to hear some of the things on the radio or television. If we had musical instruments we mightn't sing so much ourselfs. We never heard yet of any of our people stealing or getting in any trouble with the law."

I told them a story I'd heard about a man who tried to sell a car to an Old Mennonite. The farmer said he couldn't buy it because the devil was in it.

"But what about the gasoline motor you use?" the salesman asked. "It's the same thing – isn't the devil in that too?"

"Yes, but he's fastened down and I can make him do whatever I want, in a car he's running around and might get out of control."

The family laughed heartily. "That sounds chust like something old Levi Gingerich would say," David said. "He'd have an answer for anybody that tried to get smart with him."

"We take a ride in a car sometimes but it would be a danger and a temptation for our young people to own one," Bevvy explained. "Anyways we love to ride behind our horses – they go fast enough for us.

"Some things we do to stay different and separate, it makes it easier to keep our rules. We don't know why we have some of them, they were handed to us from generation to generation, they're not written down. The bishop and the preachers have to change them sometimes or make new ones, but if we don't like what they tell us we can put them out of the church and do what we think is right.

"We don't believe in converting people to our ways; we leave them alone and want to be left alone – religion should be quiet and deep in the heart, not on the tongue. We're supposed to live simple so we can have more time to think about the Lord; if we got stylish we might get proud. We could never be clever like other people anyway – we're chust farmers, we love best to watch things grow, and work makes us happy."

"We like being boss on our own land," David said with an air of unallowed pride. "I would hate to have to work for somebody else that would tell me what I should or shouldn't do."

On the last night of my stay in the fieldstone house the family sat with me on the porch waiting for the car that would come to take me away. I said, "I haven't heard a cross or grumbling word since I came here. Don't you ever get mad? Don't your children ever quarrel or disobey? Are you never tired of working? Do you never break your rules?"

They looked at one another and laughed. "We've all been extra good this week because you were here," Lyddy Ann said.

"We were telling you what all we're supposed to do but we don't always do it," Bevvy grinned.

Salome brought me a hyacinth, Grossdoddy gave me a willow whistle he'd made, Topsy pushed against my hand for a pat, there was the scent of honeysuckle and blossoms, the sound of frogs near the river.

Salome said to me, "You are so quiet now, why don't you talk?"

"I was thinking how peaceful it is here," I said.

David nodded. "That's what I often think."

"In the world I'm going back to we are always fighting for peace."

MENNONITE
MEALS

ONE OF the joys of my life is to visit my Old Order Mennonite friends the Martins in their sprawling old fieldstone farmhouse near the Conestoga River in Waterloo County. Their large old-fashioned kitchen, warmed by a big black cookstove, always has a homely fragrance of wonderful things to eat. Sometimes there is an apple smell, sometimes an aroma of rivel soup, roasting meat, baking cinnamon buns or spicy botzelbaum pie.

Bevvy, the plump little lady of the house, is always busy schnitzing, canning or cooking. With the wings of her soft brown hair smoothly parted under her organdie prayer cap she wears a plain navy-blue dress with a skirt almost down to her ankles. She greets me with a smile and a handshake: "Of course you'll stay for supper," she says as she hangs up my coat on a nail. "You know we feel real bad if you come for a wisit and don't make out a meal."

I readily accept, always and often – resigning my figure to limbo.

The food Bevvy cooks has such mouth-watering

savour that no one can resist it. Like all Mennonite cooking it is plain but divinely flavoured and different from any other. You don't have to belong to the Mennonite faith to enjoy it: everyone who has grown up in Waterloo County where Pennsylvania Dutch Mennonites settled in 1800 is devoted to sour-cream salads and the richness of Dutch apple pie. Visitors and newcomers beg for recipes that have passed from generation to generation of Mennonite housewives without being printed in a cookbook. Everyone who tastes schnitz und knepp, crusty golden pahnhaas and luscious shoo-fly pie wants to know how to prepare them.

Simplicity, economy and experience are the keynotes of Mennonite cooking. Recipes are invented to make use of everything that is grown on Waterloo County farms. Fruits are canned and pickled and made into juicy pies. Beef and ham are cured with maple smoke, pork scraps become well-seasoned sausages. Sour milk is made into cheeses, sour cream is used in fat cakes and salads. Stale bread is crumbled and browned with butter to give zest to vegetables, noodles and dumplings. Nothing is ever wasted and every meal is a feast.

"Today it gives drepsley soup, dandelion salad and fetschpatze (fat sparrows)," Bevvy tells me as she puts on a clean print apron, tying it first in front to be sure the bow is even, then pulling it round and patting it over her stomach. I sit in the rocker by the kitchen window while she bustles between the sink, the stove and the big square table covered with bright-figured oilcloth. "You don't mind if I keep on working while we visit," she says. "The curds are getting that smell I don't like round the house and I have to quick make my kochkase (cook cheese)."

She melts butter in a granite-ware kettle and into

it pours sour-milk curds which have been scalded, crumbled and ripened for three or four days. She stirs the mass till it melts to the colour of honey, adds cream and keeps stirring till it comes to a boil that goes poof! then pours it into a crock and sets it away in the pantry. "Do you want to lick the dish?" She gives me a spoon and the kettle to scrape. "Some like it better with caraway seed in but we rather have it chust plain." Sampling its mild mellow goodness, I agree that it couldn't be better.

As she works at the kitchen sink Bevvy glances through the window above it. "I look up the lane every once in a while to see if there's a horse and rig coming for supper," she says. "We love to have company drop in."

"Does it happen often?"

"Not so much during the week but every Sunday when we have service in the church nearest us people come here for dinner. Sometimes there's not so many, maybe chust a family or two but sometimes we might have thirty-five. We never know, they chust come."

"Without being specially invited?"

"Ach, our people are always welcome. They know we have plenty to eat and it don't take long to get ready when everyone helps. Come once and I'll show you."

In a dark pantry off the kitchen she shows me crocks of cheese, elderberries, lotvarrick (apple butter), bags full of schnitz, dried corn and beans, pails of maple syrup and sacks of sugar and flour.

The cellar looks like a store. A room twelve feet square has shelves all around it from the floor to the ceiling filled with quart and half-gallon jars of fruit, vegetables, jam and pickled things. On a larder that hangs from the ceiling in the centre of the room are pies and buns and cake. On the floor there are crocks of head cheese, jars of canned beef and chicken, and pork sausage sealed in with lard.

In another room smoked meats and sausages hang from the beams above us. There are great bins of potatoes and turnips. Other vegetables are stored in boxes of leaves and there are barrels full of apples.

"This is our work for the summer and fall," Bevvy says. "We like preserving and it makes us feel good when we have it away in the cellar."

When Bevvy's children come from school and their chores in the barn are all done, Amsey, aged ten, the very shy youngest in black stove-pipe pants and a collarless jacket, shines up a basket of apples, then happily makes a bowlful of popcorn because there is company to treat.

Bevvy's merry pretty daughter Lyddy Ann, who is fifteen and dressed like her mother except that she doesn't wear a cap, sets the kitchen table with ironstone china and the staples that are on it for breakfast, dinner and supper. There is bread and butter and jam: "We were taught we'd be sick if we didn't eat jam-bread at the front part of every meal," Bevvy says. There are pickles and dishes of sours: "We may never leave anything on our plates and sometimes a little relish on a piece of schpeck (fat meat) helps to make it swallow," Lyddy says. For every meal there are potatoes and coffee.

At least twice a day there's a plateful of summer sausage. For breakfast there is in addition coffee-cake, porridge or cornmeal mush and a bowlful of schnitz and gwetcha (dried apples and prunes cooked together). For dinner and supper there is always a bowl of fruit, a plateful of cookies or cake, pudding and pie – besides soup and the main course. When I tease Bevvy about having three desserts she says, "Canned peaches are not dessert, they are chust fruit.

Pudding it not dessert neither, it is only for filling the corners, and cookies and pie are chust natural for anybody to have."

On the stove there's a kettle of simmering beef broth, a pot of potatoes is boiling, ham is frying in a pan, a sauce for the salad is thickening, and in a pan of hot lard the fetschpatze are becoming a tender golden brown.

Bevvy's great handsome husband, David, wearing a plaid shirt and overalls, and her twenty-year-old Salome, dressed like Lyddy Ann, come in from milking the cows. They greet me with hearty handshakes, then wash and "comb themselves" at the sink.

At the stove there's a clatter of action. Bevvy puts the baked fetschpatze into the warming closet with the meat and potatoes. Into the beef broth she lets drip through a colander a batter of egg, milk and flour. Lyddy mixes the salad. Bevvy adds parsley to the soup and pours it into a bowl.

We sit around the bountiful table and bow our heads in a long silent prayer.

Everyone reaches for a piece of bread. The steaming soup bowl is passed among us and we ladle into our dinner plates its clear fragrant broth thickened by tiny dumplings. Bevvy says, "Grossmommy Brubacher always told me drepsley (dripped batter) soup is especially nourishing for the sick."

"But I ain't sick," David's bright brown eyes are teasing. "I guess that's why I rather would have bean soup."

"Ach, you like any thick soup where I sprinkle buttered browned bread crumbs on," Bevvy says with a smug little smile.

"Except rivel soup," Amsey reminds her. It is made from milk thickened with egg and flour rubbed into rivels (crumbs), Lyddy tells me.

"He eats that too if he has a slice of raw onion and summer sausage with," Bevvy says.

"Ach, I eat anything if I like it real good or not, that's how we are taught not to waste," David says. "What soup do you like?" he asks me.

"Any kind Bevvy makes is so thick and wonderful I can almost eat it with a fork."

"More filling than the kind you buy in the cans, hah?" David holds his spoon like a sceptre.

"Have you never tried canned soup?" I asked him.

"We never bought a can of anything yet," Bevvy answers. "We always chust make our own."

"We got more different kinds yet than they got in the stores," Salome says. "We make soup from vegetables, from meat, from leftovers, and we have all kinds of milk soups." She paused to sop up the remains of her drepsley soup with buttered bread to clean her plate for the salad. "I think we make soup out of everything you could put in your mouth to eat."

"Ach, Salome, that ain't right." Amsey looks at his sister reproachfully. "You know we never yet had soup made from huckleberry pie."

Sour cream with a bit of sugar and vinegar is the dressing for most Pennsylvania Dutch Mennonite salads. With finely chopped onion it is poured over lettuce or spinach leaves, cucumbers, boiled schnippled string beans and hot or cold cabbage.

Dandelion salad can be made only in springtime when the greens are pale and tender. In autumn Bevvy mixes curly yellow-leaved endive with the same piquant sauce – which can also be used to make hot-potato salad. She fries bits of bacon in a pan till they're crisp then takes them out and stirs a little flour into the fat. She beats an egg or two in a bowl, adds sour cream, salt, pepper and vinegar, then

34

carefully pours the mixture into the pan and stirs till it's fairly thick. When it is slightly cooled she mixes it with the dandelion and garnishes it with hard-boiled eggs and the bacon bits.

As we eat it with smoked ham and mashed potatoes Bevvy says, "The salad we like the best and easy to make for whatever crisp greens you have, is a real old-time recipe I got from David's mother. For each person to be served you fry a slice of bacon till it crackles, take it out and to the fat in the pan put one tablespoon of brown sugar, one tablespoon of vinegar and some salt and pepper; it will sizzle and spit so have care for yourself, the sugar might get kind of lumpy; let it melt, then cool it all a little before you mix in two tablespoonfuls of sour cream. Now pour it over the greens and the bacon broken in with it and on top slice eggs, tomato or radish rings or anything nice looking you got that goes good."

"Then put it quick on the table and it will soon be all," Salome adds.

"I never seen you measure it that way yet," Lyddy Ann says to her mother.

"Ach, I made it so often already I chust put in what I think. Like for most things, I tell by the feel or the taste. The way we cook got handed down from cheneration to cheneration. Since I was a little girl I helped my mam and I learned from her chust like my girls learn from me. That's why it's hard to give exact amounts of a recipe to a stranger."

Salome says, "She tells us 'put in a little handful of this, or a big handful of that, a pinch of one thing or half-an-egg-shell of something else, or a lump the size of a butternut.' It's always 'flour to stiffen or enough to make a thin batter.' And for soup and the like of that it's 'put in milk or water up to the second scratch in the kettle'!"

36

Bevvy laughs, "Ach, well, so it must be. How much you make depends on how many people you cook for. We don't like to run short on anything but we don't like to waste nothing neither."

"She usually guesses chust right," Amsey says, "except when it's brown sugar sauce for the apple dumplings and I could eat extra."

Bevvy cooks all her meats and vegetables without consulting a guide and their flavour is magnificent. She makes potpie of pigeons and rabbits and veal. She roasts beef, pork and lamb. Her gravies are brown and shiny. She fries chickens in butter and, dipped in egg and bread crumbs, the little fresh fish that Amsey catches in the river. She cooks sauerkraut with succulent spareribs. In an iron pot she makes stew and pot roasts browned with onions and bay leaves. Sometimes she has duck or roast goose bursting with savoury dressing.

"But we don't always have fresh meat in the country," Bevvy says. "Only right after we butcher. We have to cure it to keep it. Some we make into sausage, some we pack solid in jars and steam it, we smoke beef and ham. What we like best is the summer sausage: it is beef and pork ground real fine with seasoning and saltpetre, then stuffed tight in cotton bags the size of a lady's stocking and smoked for a week with maple smoke."

"We can eat that every day; we never get sick of it," David says.

"We couldn't live without summer sausage," little Amsey says as he slaps a slice on a piece of bread and butter.

"Ach, we could live without only we rather wouldn't," Bevvy says. "We got all other kinds yet, like schwadamahga sausage and liverwurst and head cheese: they're mostly made from the pork scraps

37

but they go good with fried potatoes and pickles, small corn-on-the-cob, or beet and red-cabbage salad."

Salome says, "I rather have schnitz und knepp (dried apples boiled with a ham bone and dumplings)."

"Me too," says Lyddy Ann.

"You should see these women," David turns to me, "how they sit sometimes all day schnitzing apples and drying them for the winter. Or making lot-varrick from cider and apples and cinnamon boiled and stirred half a day till it is brown and thick enough to spread with schmearkase on bread" He licks his lips and shakes his head, "Oh my, but that is good."

"She'll think we're a pig the way we make so much of our food," Salome says.

Bevvy smiles at me calmly, "She knows we work hard and we need it and never throw nothing away."

Not even a piece of bread. Before it's too stale Bevvy uses it for pudding or stuffing in tenderloin, spareribs, or fowl. She breaks pieces of bread into milk soups. When it is hard as a cracker she grinds it and keeps it in jars to mix with cheese on a casserole or to brown with butter and sprinkle over cooked vegetables, brown buttered dumplings with onions and anything made with a cream sauce.

"One of our strictest rules is never to waste a thing," Bevvy says. "When the Mennonites were over in Switzerland yet they got chased around by those that didn't like their peace-loving religion and I guess they had to eat whatever they could get. Then in 1683 they started coming to Pennsylvania and gradually had things a little easier. But those that came up here to Ontario after the American Revolution had it poor again. Even if they had money

38

they couldn't buy anything yet because there was nothing here but bush till they cleared the land and started to grow things.

"It's only lately since I grew up that we bought food in the stores except sugar and molasses, spices and salt. We only used what we grew in our own fields and garden and made recipes up to suit."

From a drawer in the cupboard Bevvy brings me her most treasured possession: a little handwritten black notebook in which she has copied recipes she has swapped and inherited. It is well-worn and some of its pages are spattered with lard or batter. At the top of each page is written the name of the recipe's donor. There is Aunt Magdaline's Hurry Cake, Grossmommy Martin's Kuddlefleck and Cantaloupe Pickle, Melinda Gingerich's Groundcherry Preserve. "When I see those names," Bevvy says, "I know chust how it tasted because most of the recipes I got when I ate at their places."

This is Cousin Katie's recipe for fetschpatze (fat sparrows, because of the odd shapes they take when spoonfuls of batter are dropped in hot lard):

> *1 beaten egg*
> *a little salt*
> *1 cup sour cream or sour milk*
> *1 round teaspoon of soda*
> *flour to stiffen*

"We eat them hot and dunked in maple syrup," Bevvy says as the fetschpatze are passed around the table. And we all eat so many that David says, "It wonders me that we'll have room after this for the pie."

Pie appears on Bevvy's table three times a day. Every Friday she and Salome bake twenty pies and store them away in the cellar. If company comes on

Sunday after church the pies may all be used at once, if not there'll be enough pies to last the week. Their variety is infinite: besides all the fruit, milk and mince pies there are sour cream raisin, tomato, cottage cheese, buttermilk, botzelbaum (somersault), and some invented on the spur of the moment to keep things from being wasted. It is not surprising that the Pennsylvania Dutch are credited with originating the double crust pie.

Dutch apple or schnitz has various versions. Sometimes Bevvy makes hers extra rich: she places the schnitz (segments of apple) close together in a pie shell; with crumbs of flour, brown sugar and butter she fills up the spaces and covers the apples, then dribbles a few spoonfuls of sour cream on top and sprinkles the pie with cinnamon. After it's baked and cooled you wish you could smell it and eat it forever.

Shoo-fly pie no doubt got its name because it tempts more than just people. Bevvy says it's a Mennonite favourite because it keeps well in a cellar. Her recipe calls for equal parts of baking molasses and water and a pinch of soda poured into an un-baked shell and covered with crumbs made of flour, brown sugar and butter. Sometimes she makes it with maple syrup and calls it candy pie. Then it's so gooey and luscious that it is ravished before it can reach the basement.

When I ask Amsey which is his favourite, he says, "Peach pie made with the peeling." Bevvy smiles apologetically, "We make it sometimes with the peelings after we did the canning. You know how sometimes the peaches don't peel too good and a little bit of flesh sticks yet? Well we chust boil it with sugar and a little water till it's almost like jam then we put it in a baked pie shell and cover it with whipped cream or boiled custard."

Amsey rolls his big brown eyes, "And that really schmecks (tastes)!" he says.

Every plate on the Martin's table is as clean as if it had not been used when we finish eating our supper. David sits back in his chair with a grunt of great satisfaction and dexterously uses a toothpick. Salome glances at me and laughs. "You look like you have afraid you'll bust your buttons."

"I am. I think I've gained five pounds since I sat down here."

"Ach, not chust from one meal," Bevvy says.

David's eyes have a teasing twinkle, "If she eats with us for a week she'd be wonderful fat."

"Like Aunt Hannah," says Amsey.

"Shame on youse," Bevvy chides, "she ain't got the frame to sit that broad."

"I'd certainly lose my waistline if I ate much of your wonderful cooking."

David grins and pats his well-rounded belly, "I'm glad our people ain't so stylish that they care about getting fat. We chust eat ourselves till we're full."

MARKET DAY IN
KITCHENER

ALMOST EVERY Saturday morning of my life in
Kitchener, Ontario, I have gone – and still go – to
the bountiful farmers' market behind the city hall,
where plump, placid women, wearing the plain
clothes and bonnets of various Amish and Mennonite sects, come – as they have come since 1839 –
to sell tiny cobs of pickled corn, apple butter, shoo-
fly pie, kochkase und kimmel (cook cheese with caraway), schwadamahga sausage, crocheted doilies, and
goose wings that are "extra goot for cleaning out the
corners."

Every Saturday, and Wednesday in the summer
and fall, I go to feast my eyes and prepare to feast
my stomach on cheeses, meat, fowl, fresh-picked
vegetables, fruits, and flowers that to me seem more
lavish and beautiful than any I have seen in the
famous markets I have visited in faraway places of
the world: Paris and Strasbourg in France, Berne
and Fribourg in Switzerland, Seville in Spain,
Caernarven in Wales, Haarlem in Holland, Mexico
City, New Orleans, and Lancaster, Pennsylvania.

Part of my preference for the produce of the
Kitchener market may be that when I have visited

markets abroad I have not been able to buy and take back to my hotel room a nice smelly piece of cheese, a bunch of crisp asparagus, a garlic-flavoured raw sausage, or a tall, blooming lilac bush to be planted. When I go to the market in Kitchener I buy until I fill up the trunk of my car; then I go home and prepare dandelion salad, schnitz und knepp (apples and dumplings), schmearkase (buttermilk curd), and Dutch apple pie, with recipes brought to Waterloo County by the Mennonite settlers 169 years ago.

Another joy of the Kitchener market is meeting friends and relatives and watching the crowd of shoppers: pert housewives in slims, shuffling old men, couples haggling in German, old-country peasant women wearing babushkas and big, flat, black shoes, goggle-eyed tourists with cameras or sketch pads, Kitchener's head librarian, Dorothy Shoemaker, blissfully absorbed by little children lost amongst adult legs. In summer I greet acquaintances on their way to the Shakespearean Festival at Stratford, and I show them where to buy gingerbread men, or smoked pork chops.

At the height of the Saturday-morning trade it is impossible to hurry (but who would want to?) through the aisles made by the long rows of tables inside the two-storey brick building, or to buck the crowds along the stands and vendors' trucks that line the outdoor platforms in spring, summer and fall. For blocks around the streets are jammed with cars, parking lots are packed solid, and traffic police try almost in vain to keep people moving.

The market opens at five in the morning and closes at two in the afternoon. I've never been there so early and I know better than to go there so late, since by noon many of the farmers have sold out and gone home. From seven until eleven o'clock is the

43

busiest time. If I ever get there before seven I'll meet my mother who doesn't want to combat the traffic that develops later; before eight I'll see my friend Mardie Broome who likes a choice of the best; or young Joe Zuber selecting delicacies for the gourmet dining-room of his father's Walper Hotel – kohlrabi, water-cress, gooseberries to stuff geese, Heidelfingen cherries for roast duckling. If I arrive after nine and want kochkase, I'm sure to be told by the Mennonite woman whose cheese I prefer, "If I hat some I'd gif you any but what I got iss all."

Hundreds of local shoppers (me among them) are regular customers at certain tables and stalls. Year after year, from childhood until old age, they go faithfully to the same farmers every week carrying bottles for cream, boxes for eggs, and bowls for kochkase in their large wicker baskets. They inspect and price other produce, and move on, to return to buy the best – or the cheapest. Though I buy regularly from certain farmers I don't know their names and I don't think they know mine – except such old-timers as Sam Roth, who only last week said to me, "I remember you from way back yet when you used to come with your ma."

In those days, drawing my little red-wheeled express wagon, I waited for my mother at the end of the long cement platform with all the kids who, by delivering customers' baskets to their homes, earned enough tiny Canadian five-cent pieces to admit them to the Roma theatre to see The Phantom Rider on Saturday afternoon. I always waited impatiently while Mother shopped and visited and eventually filled her baskets and was ready to have me pull them home as she walked alongside to steady the load and retrieve a peach or a cabbage that might bump off when the wagon went over a curb.

44

When Mother learned to run the family Nash, she drove the two blocks from our house to the market and I still had to go with her to help carry her baskets to the car. The only things that interested me in those days were the kittens and puppies sold by farm children just outside the back door, and the fluffy chicks and baby bunnies they brought for sale at Easter.

Now I go eagerly to the market because I thoroughly enjoy every bit of it. Upstairs, the variety ranges from sauerkraut to shell jewelry; most of the home baking, sewing, and handicrafts are sold there – along with comb honey, wool socks, fresh fish, home-made soap, and everything else that the vendors have grown or made themselves. Farm women with butternuts or sticky buns often bring gaily coloured hooked mats or hand-woven runners to sell. Halfway down the right aisle a blond young man has bundles of freshly dried herbs. By the backstairs is blind Peter Lipniki's popcorn machine. Against the left wall, near the front, a Mennonite woman, wearing a white organdie prayer cap, offers crisp, deep-fried "rosettes"; she tells me, "With ice cream on top and crushed berries over, they gif a dessert good enough for a funeral." At the other end of the aisle, the bearded men and pretty black-kerchiefed women of the Communal Colony of the Brethren sell pillows, noodles, and the greaseless geese that attract buyers from as far away as New York State and Detroit.

In the basement along the outside aisles are the butchers: those from the city on the left, those from the country and neighbouring villages on the right. Buyers, three deep in front of the tables, jostle one another to buy pigs' tails, Black Forest-style hams, and an incredible assortment of sausages. One German city butcher has seventy-five varieties of processed meats; many farmers sell fresh fowl, squabs, and rabbits; one country butcher sells half a ton of smoked or fresh pork sausage every week. In great demand are braunschweiger, blood-and-tongue sausage, gefuellte kalbs brust (veal stuffed with pork and green pistachios), galrich (jellied pigs' hocks) and schwadamahga sausage (a pressed mixture of chopped pork hide, heart, and head, encased in a stomach and smoked). My favourite is farmers' summer sausage. Occasionally for an old fashioned treat I buy a small piece of head cheese, to melt, spread over boiled potatoes, and eat with a sour-cream salad.

All the cheeses at the market are sold inside the building. Several vendors have limburger, Tilsit, essrum and other varieties made in Waterloo County cheese factories. Many of the farm women, along with their eggs or tatted fancies, bring a crock of kochkase und kimmel that they make every week by boiling ripened sour milk curd till it looks like congealed glue; flecked with caraway seed, it has a delicate flavour. If you don't come early to get it you'll be told, "Ach it's all already, you should haf come sooner yet." The farm women also bring balle kase: a stranger might mistake it for a ball of art gum – quite strong in flavour and smell, it delights a Pennsylvania Dutch palate.

At a table not quite midway along the left aisle downstairs, a short, plump, black-bonneted woman offers little pats of schmearkase wrapped in waxed paper, for a nickel each. I buy a quarter's worth to take home and prepare as she tells me: "You chust mix it with a little salt and plenty sweet cream till it's real extra smooth, then you put some in a nappie, pour lots of maple syrup over," she winks and smiles broadly, "and that really schmecks (tastes good)."

Throughout the market building farmers' wives sell pasteurized sour cream. The supply seldom meets the demand: no Waterloo County dinner is complete without a sour-cream salad, so easy to make. A teaspoonful of sugar, a teaspoon of vinegar, salt, pepper, and half a cupful of sour cream should be enough for three people when dribbled over tender leaf or butter lettuce, with chives or onion.

The same sour-cream dressing is wonderful on string-bean salad. I have found that a six-quart basket is just enough to satisfy ten gourmet friends from Toronto. I schnippel (french) the beans, boil them in salted water till they are barely cooked, drain, cool, and generously smother them with the thick sour-cream dressing to which I have added plenty of onion that I slice thin, sprinkle with salt, let stand for ten minutes, then squeeze (I don't know why this is done but my mother has always done it and the flavour is special). She does the same thing with peeled, thinly sliced cucumbers (discarding the juice) before adding squeezed onion and sour-cream dressing to make a super salad. I'm sorry I can't give the exact measurements – people always eat more than they think they can – I just guess, experiment, and taste till it's right, or call my mother for advice: she tells me not to use too much vinegar, the flavour should be rich and subtle, not sour, and it can't be achieved without farmers' cream.

Any Mennonite woman who sells cream at the market will tell you to use a warm sour-cream dressing for endive or dandelion salad: fry until crisp several slices of slivered bacon, remove the bits from the drippings and pour away all but two tablespoonsful of the fat; mix one teaspoon of salt, two of sugar, two of vinegar, one and a half teaspoons of flour, and a cupful of thick sour cream; pour this into the pan with the bacon fat and cook slowly till it thickens. Just as the family sits down to eat, pour the warm (not hot) mixture over the crisp, cut-up endive or dandelion, mix lightly, garnish with hard-boiled eggs and the bacon bits, and serve it with potatoes, broiled smoked pork chops, roasted pigs' tails, or farmers' browned pork sausage, with a schnitz pie for dessert.

Schnitz pie can be bought at the market from any number of well-rounded farm women who sell home baking that is hard to resist. Into a pastry-lined pie plate they place pieces of apple cut into schnitz (segments about an inch thick); over them they spread crumbs made of one cup of brown sugar, three tablespoons of soft butter, and three tablespoons of flour rubbed together. A sprinkle of cinnamon, dabs of sour cream, and the pie is ready to be baked till the apples are soft and golden. It's best served slightly warm and with cheddar.

Rich warm flavour and experience are the keynotes of these recipes which have passed from generation to generation of market vendors to market customers without finding their way into a cook book. The peace-loving Mennonites, fleeing religious persecution in Switzerland, probably brought the recipes with them to Pennsylvania in the seventeenth century and from there to Waterloo County in the early 1800's.

When these hard-working pioneers had cleared the forest and were able to grow more than they needed for themselves, they traded what they could in the stores and in 1839 started selling the rest of their surplus in an open area near the main street of the village of Berlin (now Kitchener) as farmers still do on market day in Switzerland's cities. In 1869 Jacob Y. Shantz, an enterprising Mennonite, succeeded in establishing a year-round market in the basement of the building which housed the village council chamber and the post office.

The market quickly outgrew its quarters and spread out round the building till a separate structure – the present one – was erected in 1907. Most of the vendors in the early days were Mennonites and bearded Amish farmers who, in winter, came in cutters with sleighbells ringing, their wives and children bundled to their eyes in shawls and cowhide robes; in summer they came in topless buggies or wagons, their wives wearing stiff black bonnets over white prayer caps, and clean print aprons over their modestly long cotton dresses – exactly as they do now.

Through the years the market kept changing. Butchers and other Waterloo County farmers rented tables beside those leased by the Mennonites and Amish. In the late 20's a long cement platform took the place of some of the horse-stalls that were no longer needed because many of the farmers were driving to the market in automobiles. In the night, truckers came from the Niagara Peninsula and waited till the five o'clock opening bell rang to unload their fruit – sometimes resorting to fist fights to determine who got the best places.

Now there are also farmers who emigrated from Holland, Germany, Hungary, England – and more Mennonite farmers than ever – selling produce at the Kitchener market. Though the Mennonites can be distinguished from other vendors by the modest simplicity of their clothes and the bonnets of their women, most of them have given up the ancient prohibitions and the shawls of the Old Order. Only one family now comes regularly in a buggy – except in early spring when four or five Old Order Mennonites with maple syrup to sell tie their horses to the few hitching rings left on the wall beside the city hall.

The market changes with the changing seasons. In January and February only a few vendors use the outdoor platforms; everyone else crowds into the building. Old Mrs. Kieswetter, walking like a queen, comes every week with her bowl to buy kochkase; Mrs. Czezuliki, wearing mink and plaid slacks, always comes for root vegetables and house plants. One farm woman wouldn't miss coming to market though she has only a pot of cooked navy beans, four quarts of onions, and half a dozen bottles of fresh horse-radish for sale. Other farm women who have no grown things to sell in winter, bring home-made bread, fastnachts (raised doughnuts), and dried schnitz.

The sight of schnitz at the market on a cold winter day suggests a warm steamy Mennonite kitchen with a couch in a corner, a table set with ironstone china, and a big, black, wood-burning cook-stove with a ham bubbling slowly. Before the ham is cooked off the bone, two cups of schnitz, two tablespoonsful of brown sugar, and water which has been used to cover and soak the schnitz overnight, are added and cooked for an hour. Then the knepp (dumplings) are dropped in, covered tightly, and cooked for twelve minutes without lifting the lid. The ham, schnitz und knepp are then served with potatoes, hot cole-slaw, or bean salad, and shoo-fly pie for dessert.

From the middle of blustery March I start looking at the market for pussy willows and the first maple syrup. That's when my mother used to make her own version of shoo-fly pie, so chewy and sweet we called it candy pie. Into an unbaked pie shell she poured a cupful of maple syrup dissolving half a teaspoon of soda; over it she spread crumbs made with brown sugar, flour and butter – as for schnitz pie. While the pie was baking to a rich, warm brown, the luscious sticky goo usually ran over into the oven. The Mennonite women at the Kitchener market make their shoo-fly pie by pouring half a cup each of dark molasses and boiling water mixed with half a teaspoon of soda between several layers of crumbs; the result looks rather dry and cakey but they say it's a favourite because it stays moist for a week.

The market looks like a garden when spring comes. Smiling farm women dig sprouting perennials from their gardens and sell them with plenty of earth round the roots. Almost every table in the building has pailsful of flowers: violets, bleeding hearts, honey-suckle, old-fashioned green and yellow double daffodils, apple blossoms, lily-of-the-valley. On the outdoor platforms hopeful gardeners flit from flats of seedlings to baskets of pansies and petunias, to rose bushes, shrubs, trees, raspberry canes, and almost anything you can think of that will grow in this part of the world.

Early summer at the Kitchener market gets me out of bed with the sunrise to be there in time to buy fruit and vegetables while the dew is still on them – I like to think. Because they're so perfect and fresh I always buy too many berries and cherries – but never quite enough tender garden peas, since I always manage to shell and eat half of my basketful before I reach home.

From the time that the strawberries ripen and until the last grapes disappear in the fall there is a market on Wednesday mornings as well as on Saturday. It is not so well stocked or attended; the upstairs of the building is unused, but there is less traffic congestion, and the outside platforms have the same thrilling abundance.

As summer progresses the colours of the market change from delicate shades to the bold ones of marigolds and delphinium. The tables are loaded with bushels of cucumbers, melons, and corn. Families come to carry fruits and pickles for mamma to can and make into relishes and jam. I run back and forth many times to my car with baskets of tomatoes, peaches, and yellow transparents that make the best applesauce.

There is a mellow air of thanksgiving as fall comes to the market with sweet cider, grapes that make wine, pumpkins, wild mushrooms, and weirdly shaped gourds, everlasting straw flowers, purple plums and big winter pears.

From the end of November the market begins to look like a Christmas bazaar as the farmers' wives display the work of their ever-busy hands: crocheted baskets stiffened with sugar, knitted mitts, scarves, and tuques, cushion tops, dolls' clothes, aprons, smocked dresses for little girls; there are innumerable (and awful) novelties made of styrofoam, ribbons and lace, driftwood centrepieces and decorations for mantels, Indian baskets, carved wood and leather goods. The Christmas baking is irresistible: hard round pfeffernüsse, anise-flavoured lebkuchen, springerle with bas-relief pictures pressed on their pale tops, and thousands of cookies shaped like stars, trees, bells, Santa Claus, and Kriss Kringle.

People often say to me, "Why do you go to the market every week? You can buy just as well at the stores."

I tell them the market is much more exciting, more sociable, and more fun. The Kitchener market is marvellous; nowhere else in the world that I've seen is there such fresh, clean, lush profusion. It gives me a feeling of security, abundance, and anticipation of joy. It gives me deep satisfaction. It has only one drawback: if I'm not careful, my overindulgence in its rich luscious foods could make me as round and "wonderful fat" as some of the happy Old Mennonites are.

THE OLD ORDER
AMISH

MEN WITH bushy Old Testament-like beards and long Dutch-cut hair under broad-brimmed black hats are often seen on the main streets of Kitchener, Waterloo, and Stratford. They wear "barn-door" britches (buttoned across the top without zippers or flies); their suit coats, fastened by hooks and eyes, have no pockets, buttons, collars, or lapels. Their women wear coal-scuttle bonnets and long, plain dresses secured by invisible pins. Bundled in shawls, they ride imperturbably in topless buggies behind their plump horses while the world rushes by all around them.

These strange people are the peace-loving Old Order Amish (pronounced Ahmish). By shunning conventional ways and trying to live as their ancestors did in 1525, they insulate themselves from the age of sputniks, tension, and speed, and find everlasting security in their faith, their families, and their prosperous farms in Waterloo and Perth counties.

They spurn everything modern. If they buy farms with well-appointed houses they tear out electric wiring and bathroom fixtures, remove oil furnaces and telephones. They won't own a radio or a television set; musical instruments are taboo. They don't go to movies, will turn their backs on a camera, wouldn't ride in a plane. When asked why they won't buy a car, truck, or tractor, they reply, "Because the Lord didn't drive one when he lived on earth."

Not even the laws of the country can force the Old Amish to violate the teaching of Jacob Amman, the Swiss Mennonite preacher who founded the sect in 1693 by exhorting his followers to return to the ways of the Mennonite martyrs at the time of the Swiss Reformation. They won't go to court, won't swear an oath – and their word is accepted as their bond. They won't take up arms in a war – and Canadian law has exempted them. Though they pay taxes they refuse Old Age pensions and Family Allowances – that might obligate them to the government and make them less independent. They won't vote in federal or provincial elections – they say they are too dumb. Their children stop school on the day they are fourteen because higher education might lead them away from the flock.

By being different and separate the Old Amish claim to obey the biblical precept, "Be ye not conformed to this world." Anything that is modern or fashionable they consider as worldly, therefore the work of the devil and not for their use or enjoyment – but all right for anyone else. The Old Amish are humble, hard-working folk who quietly mind their own business and make no attempt to convert other people.

Unlike modern church organizations with their ever-expanding buildings, Ontario's ten congregations of Old Order Amish – about 1000 people – have no church buildings at all. For worship the Old Order gather in each other's houses or barns and through services three hours long sit on backless benches that are taken from one meeting place to another in a horse-drawn wagon. They are sometimes called House or Barn Amish – (to distinguish them from the more numerous and progressive Church Amish-Mennonites). Their preachers, chosen for life by lot from slips of paper drawn from a Bible, are farmers with no ministerial training but the reading of the Holy Book and the stern Amish code based on the Bible's literal interpretation.

Obedience to their rules is severely imposed. If a baptized member of the sect fails to comply with its various regulations he – or she – is liable to be "placed in the ban." He is excommunicated from the church, not allowed to eat at the table with his family or sleep in bed with his spouse; fellow church members do not drink or eat with him or take anything from his hand until he repents of his sins, and is allowed back into the congregation by a vote of the members.

Rigid austerity is the rule of the Old Order Amish. Upholstered comfort and decoration are not allowed in their homes: floors have no carpeting, windows have no drapes or frilled curtains, walls have no pictures or paper.

The style of Old Amish clothing, prescribed by the traditions of their sect, has not changed in three hundred years. The men's coats are buttonless as a protest against the ornamented uniforms of medieval militia; that too is why the married men wear beards but no moustaches, and parting and clipping their hair is prohibited. Not to be tempted by fashion, the women wear clothes made from an identical pattern; cosmetics and jewelry – including wedding-rings – are forbidden. Their hair, never cut or curled, is centre-parted and drawn tightly into a knob, always covered by a kerchief, an organdie cap tied under the chin, or a coal-scuttle bonnet – because women's heads should be covered when they pray and they might pray at any time and anywhere.

Though the Old Amish look pious and have many self-imposed deprivations, they seem to enjoy life. They love getting together to talk; every Sunday they visit each other by the dozen; hundreds of them gather at auction sales, barn raisings, funerals, and wedding feasts. At their quiltings and at the Sunday night singings for their teenagers they have hilarious fun; they play boisterous games and are practical jokers. With bags full of treats they love to go on a train to visit American relatives.

About 50,000 Old Order Amish live in the United States. In Pennsylvania, where they first settled when they left Europe, they are the most colorful part of the Pennsylvania Dutch culture and are advertised as a tourist attraction. Many books and stories have been written about them; a musical comedy, "Plain and Fancy", has been most successful; their images and folk art appear on greeting cards, pottery and souvenirs. Amish delicacies – shoo-fly pie, seven sours, and dried corn soup – are served in the restaurants of Lancaster county. But the Old Amish who live in Ontario are unexploited and almost unknown.

One day I drove twenty miles north-west from Kitchener to the heart of the Old Amish country where the fields are rich with manure, the houses are large but undistinguished, and the names on the mail boxes are a frequent repetition of Keupfer, Albrecht, Nafziger, Jantzi and Zehr.

In the villages of Milverton and Millbank, where the Amish farmers shop and do business, I encountered an attitude of respect and kindly amusement at Old Amish customs. I was told that despite their

strict rules the Old Amish do some things that seem
not unworldly. They make and drink cider and beer;
some smoke cigarettes. Though they don't own cars
they will ride in them. They'll enjoy a non-Amish-
man's radio, they will "borrow" his phone. Some
turn up regularly at a neighbour's house to watch
television; they laugh loudly at the commercials;
some like the fights, others prefer ballet and opera,
one red-bearded Amishman never misses a ball
game.

"Inconsistent?" a Milverton business man said to
me. "They're only human. You couldn't find better
neighbours."

"They never get into any trouble," a gray-haired
bystander told me. "Some of the young ones might
like to kick over the traces but the old ones keep
them in line."

"Sometimes I envy them," the businessman mused.
"They seem to have real contentment."

To find out how they achieved it I spoke to an
Old Amish bishop who had retired from farming
but still performed his church duties of marrying,
baptizing, banning and burying. He was a short,
square man with a smiling round face surrounded by
black whiskers. He wore dark overalls and rubber
boots that came up to his knees. He told me very
kindly that the Old Order Amish do not like publicity and he was afraid his people would criticize
him if he gave information about them. He said all
their ways that seem strange to outsiders were direct
biblical commands or could be traced to the days
when their ancestors were persecuted in Europe.
"And if you want to know about that you can read
it in books," he said as he turned his broad back and
strode firmly away from me.

I called on a young Amish couple who seemed

delighted to have me come to stay with them to learn how they live, but when I went back three days later they said their parents had told them not to have me and I'd better go to some of the old ones who were wiser.

They directed me to the home of Sam and Leah Keupfer, an Old Amish couple who live in a doddy house (grandfather's house), a few rooms attached to the large old farmhouse they once occupied but – according to Old Amish custom – have now given over to their youngest son and his family. Leah, a wiry little woman, 82, wearing a black dress and apron with a black kerchief tied under her chin, invited me eagerly into her small kitchen-living-room which seemed to be filled by her husband, Sam, as he stomped around in his barn boots, his patriarchal beard and long grizzled hair streaming under a great, dusty black hat.

"Sit you, sit you," he welcomed me and gestured with his enormous, work-hardened hand towards several plain wooden chairs lined up against the green painted walls. The room had no drapes, no pictures, and no paper on its walls, no floor-covering but a piece of linoleum and a handmade rag mat. There was nothing unuseful but flowering plants in tin cans on the window sills and bits of cherished cheap china and glass tucked away in a large corner cupboard.

With his knees wide apart the old man sat on a hard black leatherette couch while his wife kept moving back and forth between a dry sink and an oilcloth-covered table. "You'll haf to excuse me if I keep working," she smiled at me, "but one of ours is in the hospital and I'm making a meal to send over for her man and the kids. Our Joe is coming to fetch it."

"The word of God teaches us that we should all help each other." Sam was a retired preacher.

"That way we got nothing to worry us," Leah said, "if we get sick or old our children and relations will take care of us, if we get poor off they will feed us; if a widow loses her man our men will take in her crops and help with her chores." Leah smiled securely. "The good Lord looks after us good."

"What if something happens that wipes people out, like a fire or storm?" I asked.

"The word of God teaches us that when one member suffers all the rest suffer with him," Leah said.

"We have our property and stock valued and when there's a loss we all pay enough to cover it according to how much we've got," Sam explained. "It's just like insurance only because we pay after the loss, we have no money on hand and are not a company and it is not a gamble. All the two or three thousand Church Amish in Ontario and ourselves are in it together, so no one has to pay very much and maybe only every few years."

At the shiny coal-burning cook stove Leah lifted the lid of a large iron kettle where smoked ham and dried apple segments (schnitz) were simmering; she gently dropped in some dumplings (knepp). "I'll keep enough out for our dinner and you can stay with us," she offered me, a stranger.

The sound of a tractor in the lane sent her to the window in a flury of pleasant excitement. "Here's Joe already," she announced.

A man, bearded, long-haired, and in Old Amish clothes, came in and talked with his parents in the Pennsylvania Dutch dialect. When the dumplings were cooked Leah ladled the schnitz und knepp into a pot. Instead of handing it to her son she put the pot on the doorstep and he picked it up from there to take it away on his clattering machine.

Old Sam sensed the question in my mind. Embarrassed, he explained, "Our Joe married a woman that belongs to a congregation of Old Order that decided if God created man smart enough to make tractors He must have wanted them to be used." Sam looked stern. "We don't think it's right and we don't have much to do no more with that bunch of our people."

"Except our Joe," Leah added.

"We believe if people let all these new contraptions do their chores for them they won't have enough work to keep them busy and safe from trouble," Sam said.

"And we ain't bothered with salesmen; we just tell them what they got is against our rules," Leah told me.

Sam grinned. "A vacuum cleaner peddler came here one day and Leah says to him, 'It's no use showing it to us,' but he got his machine together anyhow. And did we ever laugh when he looked around and said, 'Where do I plug it in?' He left pretty quick and there ain't none been around since."

Leah set the table with horn-handled knives, three-tined steel forks and unmatched china. Sam dipped water from the stove's reservoir into a basin, washed his hands and face, took off his hat, combed his long hair and beard, then sat at the head of the table. We bowed our heads silently till he sighed and said heartily, "Reach for whatever you like," and helped himself first to the dumplings.

After dinner Leah took me through a door that led into the main house where her twenty-six-year-old son Noah lived with his wife, Catherine, and

63

their children Christian and Magdalena, aged three and four. The pregnant little wife, wearing glasses and the plain garb of the Old Order, welcomed me to her brown varnished kitchen. The children giggled shyly and hid their heads behind her skirts till she said, smiling, "Ach you sillies, go and play once." Then they leaned over the woodbox beside the stove and peeked at me under their arms. The pretty little girl's shapeless dark gray flannel dress was covered by a navy blue apron, her hair was slicked into tight narrow braids tied together with string; the little boy wore a home-made collarless shirt and long Old Amish britches.

"We're awful fond of our mommies and don't like to get too far away from them." Catherine explained why the Old Amish live in settlements. "I guess we never get over it, even when we get old." She smiled fondly at Leah, who added, "Besides we don't like to have to drive our horses too far for divine service and to visit each other or to help with the threshing and butchering, or if somebody's sick."

"And it's better for us to be all-together-like to keep our own ways," Catherine added.

"You live so close to town," I said, "do none of your people ever leave home to get jobs there?"

Leah looked shocked. "They daren't. Not if they do what the Lord says. They got to be farmers. It says it right in the scriptures that we should look after the earth."

"We wouldn't know how to do anything else," Catherine said, "and we wouldn't want to. We love making things grow."

Her husband, a slight man with bright eyes, came in and smiled at me shyly. "Noah has been plowing," Catherine told me; "it takes him longer than those that got tractors but he loves to walk with his horses."

Noah sat on a wooden rocking chair, rolling a cigarette while both children ran to him and perched on his knees. Leah excused herself to go back to the doddy house to get on with her work. The children giggled and chattered. "Listen those kids jabbering in German," Catherine laughed. "They can talk English as good as we can. When we're alone we talk either the one or the other so they'll know both when they get to school."

"Ours ain't the High German," Noah explained to me, "it's the Pennsylvania Dutch like the Mennonites talk."

'Only it's just a little different yet," his wife said. "My grandfather told me his grandmother used to speak French."

"But they talked German too, because in the early days they got chased pretty well all over that part of Europe," Noah told me.

He explained that the Amish are an offshoot of the Mennonites whose creed began when the establishment of a state church in Switzerland was opposed in 1525 by a group of scholars who wanted religious freedom. Members of the sect for many years suffered great persecution, torture and exile; always resisting, never fighting, they fled from one place to another. They were still having trouble when, in 1693, Jacob Amman, a young Mennonite preacher living in Alsace, got the notion that the church was lacking in discipline and urged his followers to return to the ways of its earliest martyrs. He preached that the faithful should not be yoked in marriage or in organizations with unbelievers and revived the practice of "Meidung" (the ban). Amman's separation from the Mennonite church spread into north Switzerland and Germany and soon was carried to Pennsylvania.

"The first Amishman that came to Canada was from Bavaria," Noah told me in his low drawling voice. "He landed in New Orleans in 1822 and walked most of the way to Waterloo County where he picked out some wilderness that he thought would make a good place for a colony. Then he went to the Governor of Upper Canada to ask him if it would be all right to bring people over here. The governor said, 'Go ahead,' but the Amishman was taking no chances, he went right to the palace of the King of England and got it in writing with a gold seal that the land would really be his."

Catherine smiled, "Then people came over and had families and spread out and that's how we're here."

The young couple and I chatted all afternoon. They asked me innumerable questions: how old I was, what I did in town, what I thought of taxes. The young woman showed me the man's *muhtze*, a tail coat, which was made of dark serge and would probably last him for church services, weddings, and funerals as long as he lived – 'Unless he gets fat," she laughed. She showed me her black bonnet and the dainty white organdie prayer cap with its finely pleated back that the little girl wears for church.

They told me that the preaching is held every other week in the homes of church members. The men sit on one side of the room, the women on the other. A song leader starts off the unaccompanied hymns; there are two or three sermons by the preachers and bishop. There are no church dues, the deacon collects the offerings and the money is put in the bank and distributed when it is needed among the poor of the congregation.

"But we don't have many that's poor off," Noah said, "or rich either."

"We got one that has plenty." Catherine grinned impishly at Noah.

He laughed and explained to me, "Our main aim is to raise good crops and fine cattle and to save money to buy farms for our children so they can get a good start when they marry, but this man has only one daughter and she's an old maid."

"She's only a couple years older than we are," Catherine told me, "and before we were married she tried to get Noah."

I called at the sprawling brick house of the Amishman who owned fifty cows and all the land along one mile of road. When I knocked at the door it was opened by a sullen-faced older woman who reluctantly let me come in. She looked disapprovingly at my gray kidskin coat and said, "I suppose that is mink?" Her daughter, twenty-eight, wearing the little prayer cap of the unmarried girls, was sweeping the large kitchen floor; the mother took the broom from her and thrust viciously under the stove.

"Ach mama, I wish you wouldn't do that," the girl said. "You know if you work hard you'll be sick again."

The mother glowered as she swept round the chair that I sat on. "I can't sit around when there's work to be done."

Neither woman spoke to me voluntarily. The girl put two old-fashioned irons to heat on the stove; the mother emptied a basin of water into a slop pail, then pulled on a pair of rubber boots, folded a shawl over her head and said, "I'll hunt the eggs." She gave the girl a look that said, "You be careful."

While her mother was gone the daughter was more friendly. She told me that though she hates going to the nearby cities of Kitchener, Waterloo and Stratford, she had once enjoyed a trip by car to Indiana to visit some Old Amish there. She showed me the embroidered patches of a "friendship quilt" she was collecting, and a crocheted pineapple pincushion she had made for her dower chest. She told me of the Sunday night "Singings" where the young people gather to get acquainted and to learn the complicated hymn tunes of their people. But when I asked her about the pairing-off games they play, she snapped, "We don't tell about that," and busily ironed a flannelette petticoat without speaking to me for a while.

Then, "Would you like to look at our hymn book?" she asked me.

She brought me a copy of the Ausbund, the oldest Protestant church hymnal in use in America, compiled in 1564 and written by martyrs awaiting their death. It is printed in German without music, its tunes having passed orally from generation to generation, defying both rhythm and time. Some of its hymns have as many as seventy-four verses and take over an hour to sing in the doleful one-part drone that sounds like the chanting of monks. Some of the hymns are long discourses on doctrine. Hymn 140, with thirty-two long stanzas, describes in detail the story of Hans Haslibach of Berne, his imprisonment and torture and the prophecy that at his death three signs would prove his innocence: when his head would be severed from his body it would leap into his hat, the sun would turn red and the town pump would flow crimson. Another hymn describes the trial and death of Michael Sattler, an ex-monk turned preacher, who because he had opposed infant baptism and warfare had his tongue cut out; his body, pinched and torn with red-hot tongs, was then burned at the stake.

It seems that the tenacious way in which the Old Order's refusal to conform has been maintained in compact agricultural-industrial areas probably comes from the strong sense of martyrdom that is seared into their memories, holding them together and making them look with apprehension and disapproval at the wicked ways of the "world."

The girl told me that the Old Amish used to make their own coffins but now they get them from the undertaker and sometimes they're a little too fancy. She said the casket is taken on a horse-drawn wagon to the graveyard and there it is buried by the relatives of the deceased. There are no monuments in the cemetery. The graves are marked with small slabs on which are engraved only the two initials of the dead. There are no family plots: "There's just rows and rows," the girl said. "One for little children and babies, one for half-grown kids, one for single people, one for married ones that ain't old, and one for the old folks."

She folded a towel she had ironed and put it away in a drawer. She kept looking out the window toward the road as she worked, seemingly hopeful that someone might come up the long lonely lane.

Finding marriage partners among the Old Amish is not always easy. Their numbers are limited, first cousins may not marry, no converts are sought, and every year a few young people are ex-communicated for choosing mates from the progressive Church Amish-Mennonites on neighbouring farms. But courtship is greatly encouraged, hopeful young visits are exchanged between the American and Ontario Old Orders, and the sect is increasing through the natural growth of large families.

I called back at the farm of the Keupfers several months after my first visit there. Leah was outside

on a ladder cleaning the windows of the doddy house
– though it was a cold day in January. "Sam's in the
barn," she called to me. "Go in to Catherine. I'll
come when I finish."

In Catherine's kitchen a new baby lay sleeping
in a spooled wooden cradle near the stove. "He played
a trick on me." Catherine leaned over him fondly.
"He came already before Noah could hitch up the
horse and go for the doctor to drive me to town to
the hospital."

Catherine welcomed me happily. "But you'll
have to excuse me if my place ain't fit for company
and if I keep working. I've got yet to trim wicks and
wash all the lamp chimneys. We're getting ready for
the preaching here on Sunday and everything's got
to be cleaned."

"Then I shouldn't bother you," I said.

"You're no bother. It's not like getting ready for
a wedding or a funeral; we don't feed them much –
just bread and butter and jam and apple butter and
cheese."

"How many will come?"

"Ach now, I don't know right," Noah said from
the rocking chair where he held little Magdalena on
his knee. "We don't keep church records but I think
we've got anyway eighty members in our congregation, don't you, Catherine? Then there's all the
small children and those that aren't baptized yet. It
makes quite a bunch; we set up the benches all
through the downstairs of the house."

"Isn't it hard keeping all the little ones quiet
during the long service?"

"Oh no," Catherine said. "Those women that have
small ones sit in the kitchen where they can get easy
'out back' and sometimes in the second sermon we
slip kids a cookie or a hard candy. But they have to

70

learn to behave just like we do. That's good for them."

"Our children got to learn early to do what they're told," Noah said as he fondled the little girl who had fallen asleep in his arms. "As soon as they're old enough they each get their own chores to do round the barn and the hen-house. Magdalena's helping her mother already in the kitchen. When they're fourteen they quit public school and start working full time to learn how to farm and keep house. We believe the best way to keep out of trouble and happy is to keep always busy."

"Don't you sometimes envy the people who do all the things and have all the things that you're not allowed?"

The young couple looked at each other. Noah spoke. "We got the Lord's blessing and our home and our children and our farm nearly paid for, and we got all our friends and relations near us and nothing to worry about. What more could we want?"

Catherine said, "We're contented just like we are."

KITCHENER AND
WATERLOO

KITCHENER AND Waterloo, in the fertile heart of western Ontario, consider themselves the finest pair of cities ever raised on sauerkraut and enterprise. Kitchener is the most highly industrialized community in Canada, and Waterloo, with two dynamic universities and the head offices of six insurance companies, deals with more money and more brains than any city its size in the country. Both communities are friendly and lively and solid, cautious and daring; proud of their tidy streets and well-kept houses, their music, beer, and many churches, the plump and placid woman in sombre shawls and bonnets who sell schmearkase and shoo-fly pie at Kitchener's Saturday morning market.

Situated (they claim) "in North America's belt of maximum energy," they have a healthful, high, dry climate and artesian wells of the purest water. They are served by both national railways, a network of highways, and Ontario's 500 mile Macdonald-Cartier Freeway. One quarter of Canada's population is within three hours by road from the doors of their highly productive factories; the seaway is only 35 miles away. A golden horseshoe of surrounding communities makes the Twin Cities a target for sprees of shopping, culture, and fun.

Though overwhelmed by K-W hospitality, visitors sometimes tactlessly enquire where they can swim and where there's a view. They are quickly shown the vivid blue of Kitchener's municipal pools, and how Waterloo has dammed up Laurel Creek; for scenery they are told to see the rolling hills and fruitful Mennonite farms of Ontario's fairest county, and lakes that have been dug in the large civic parks where there are picnics, band concerts and canoeing – if the lakes haven't been drained to have their bottoms cleaned.

Both cities have a passion for cleanliness and order. Upkeep is a duty sacred to all. Anyone driving around on a long summer evening will see people painting their houses and manicuring their green velvet lawns: on Brubacher Street the family of Fritz Herschenbaum, rubber worker, may be decorating a porch; on John Boulevard, Tom Seagram, whose millionaire grandfather started distilling v.o., may be seen mowing his grass; on fashionable Stanley Drive, Brigadier Walter Bean, o.b.e., Honorary Colonel of the Highland Fusiliers of Canada, and president of the Waterloo Trust and Savings Company, might be snipping sprigs off his hedges.

They boast that Kitchener is the birthplace of Hydro, of Canada's past perennial prime minister, Mackenzie King, and of one of Ontario's Lieutenant-Governors, the late Louis Breithaupt, whose grandfather started a tannery with only ninety dollars. Waterloo boasts that it has sponsored the greatest annual band festivals in America and its older housewives can make hasenpfeffer that is unexcelled in the Commonwealth.

Both cities have a dialect that is humorous and

infectious: until recent years children of totally English parentage were likely to come home from school with the inflection of the Pennsylvania Dutch and expressions like "Come here once," or "The butter iss all already," and "I got to comb my hairs yet."

Modest fortunes are made in Kitchener and Waterloo because in the 1800's freedom-loving Germans came with little but a carpet-bag of tools, a pair of skilful hands and the determination to build a stable way of life in which to raise a family. Many of the factories begun in those early days have grown with the families; the tradition of a man with a trade starting a business by himself has continued in the community to the present day. As a result, Kitchener and Waterloo have several vast industries and a diversity of manufacturers that makes them as solid as a successful department store: a falling off of sales in a furniture factory has little effect on plants that make pickle barrels, TV sets, or cookies.

K-W savings run high, people are thrifty and above all things love their homes. More than eighty-seven per cent own the houses they live in. There are few houses to rent and no slum areas; early city bylaws prohibited frame construction. There are no fabulous mansions – Twin City millionaires are too modest, or too philanthropic to be ostentatious – but there are many large new houses that look like magazine ads, and the homes of factory workers are as neat and square and solid as those of factory owners.

Though called Twin Cities they are more like a happily married couple: Kitchener, with a population of over 100,000, is the industrious, organizing male; Waterloo, with 35,000 is the quiet homemaker who, refusing amalgamation, coyly cherishes her independence and shares her partner's institutions. Waterloo's babies are born in Kitchener and her dead are buried there: her cemeteries and hospitals are in Kitchener; so are her railway station, telegraph office, art gallery and bus depot. People from both cities support the same federated charities, belong to the same clubs, play together in the K-W Symphony Orchestra, K-W Little Theatre, K-W Operatic, and Chamber Music Societies. They frequently combine their statistics – but not their brass bands or their sports: each band gives its own weekly concert, Waterloo has her own hockey arena and so has Kitchener; both have their own baseball fields – there's often a fight when K-W teams compete but they root for one another when an outside team plays either one.

When citizens speak of their home town they mean both Kitchener and Waterloo. They seldom know when they've gone from one city into the other. The communities that started as hamlets two miles apart have grown into each other so completely that connecting streets have signs at their curbs with "You are now entering Waterloo" on one side and "Welcome to Kitchener" on the other. The K-W border crosses streets in the middle of blocks, bisects the head office of the Mutual Life Assurance Company (claimed by Waterloo) and divides people's lawns and houses; a family on one side of a dining-room table might be eating sauerkraut in Kitchener while those on the other side are savouring it in Waterloo.

King Street runs through both cities like a spinal column. Kitchener's east end of it is bordered by luxurious motels, a hodge-podge of stores, restaurants, used-car lots, Dare's cookie factory and Resurrection College; it passes a Mennonite church, garages, a municipal golf club and public gardens

75

where brides have their pictures taken beside the goldfish and lily pools. The main shopping area is narrow and active, flanked by stores with shining vitrolite faces, old business blocks and a number of new ones. Farther on there are factories, offices, and clinics, the Kitchener Collegiate, K-W Hospital, and TV station.

Then, in the middle of a block, King Street is in Waterloo, with houses and factories, the Mutual Life, the gracious white clapboard Kumpf home built in 1835. The street bends northward at a United Church and Carling's brewery, passes Waterloo Square, several blocks of stores, shops, and more houses, till King Street becomes Highway 85 and runs past Martin's Meeting House where the black-shawled Old Order Mennonites come with their horses and buggies for Sunday morning services.

The Mennonite pioneers, trekking from Pennsylvania in their Conestoga wagons, followed the line of King Street when it was a swampy Indian trail through the forest a hundred and seventy years ago. The Mennonites wanted land under British rule that would give them security for their families and the religion that made them plain and independent people. In their ox-drawn wagons it took them months to come through the Allegheny Mountains, the unbridged Niagara River and treacherous Beverly Swamp to the wolf-howling wilderness they had bought in Waterloo County.

In 1806 Benjamin Eby, Abraham Weber and Joseph Schneider came to the Sand Hills and Abraham Erb settled in a cedar swamp two miles farther north. Other Mennonite settlers followed. There were land-clearing bees and building bees till each family had a log cabin. Joe Schneider built a sawmill, Abe Erb put up a grist mill, and Ben Eby built a meeting hall and a little schoolhouse. The Sand Hills grew into Ebytown with a blacksmith shop and a tavern.

John Hoffman and Sam Bowman walked up from Pennsylvania; they were seventeen years old, had fifty cents between them, and wanted to start a furniture factory. They went to Benjamin Eby, the Mennonite bishop, teacher, and farmer; he said, "All right, boys, I'll give you all the land you need; go up the road and start to build." So Kitchener's industrial career was begun.

People from Germany came to the Mennonite hamlet in 1824 and Ben Eby changed its name to Berlin to make them feel at home. Dr. John Scott and some Methodists moved in and were looked to for leadership because they spoke English and knew the laws of Canada West.

In 1835 Heinrich Peterson had a printing press hauled from Philadelphia to Berlin by a yoke of oxen. In one of the first editions of his German weekly Canada Museum he said: "No news from Germany is recorded, no important news from England, and the news from the United States is so unpleasant to relate it would bring happiness to none. It is therefore deleted." The editor's local coverage was no more favourable: he told that two young Berliners were injured while chasing deer on horses and warned that it should be an example for all reckless young men, adding somewhat glumly, "Unfortunately our warning is not much help with the young people of today. One could believe this is the age of self-wisdom, and nobody desires to take advice."

Still, Berlin kept on making progress. It had 25 houses and John Hoffman built 50 more. People moved in. A bell on John Hoffman's factory called them to fires, weddings, and work. A post office was opened in Davidson's general store and a stage coach brought mail every week. A trip in the stage coach from Preston, nine miles away, took only two hours and was gradually becoming less dangerous, though the land between and around the wilderness settlements was dense bush and marshland. Berlin citizens were often urged to arm themselves and meet at the schoolhouse to engage in a wolf or bear hunt.

Canada's first lager beer brewery was opened in Berlin in 1840. At the same time in Waterloo, David Kuntz was making bricks with which he built a brewery; he made his own beer kegs, brewed his own beer and delivered it himself in a wheelbarrow for six cents a quart. His business flourished: today, as Carling Breweries Limited, it pays millions of dollars annually in taxes to the federal and provincial governments.

In 1850 the County of Waterloo was organized. Galt, with a population of 2000, naturally expected to be made the County Town and was outraged when Berlin, with less than 800 people, put in a claim. The Galt Reporter savagely attacked the upstarts in Berlin. That spurred them on. They organized a campaign: with music, parades, and sumptuous banqueting they entertained the member of Parliament for the district and won him to their side; Frederick Gaukel, a popular tavern-keeper, offered to give two and a half acres of land between Queen and Frederick Streets for the county buildings; a monster petition was sent to the government in Toronto.

In March, 1852, the authorities announced that Berlin had been chosen to be the county seat. Poor Galt!

Berlin, with a population of 1000, was incorporated as a village two years later. Wilhelm Kaiser opened a beer garden where citizens enjoyed their lager on summer evenings and listened to the playing of Berlin's first German Band. The village now had four taverns, nine church congregations, and a singing society. It had four wood-working shops, a tannery, a foundry, a soap-chandlery, a pottery, two brickyards, wagon shops, smithies and saddleries, five weavers' handlooms and a hatmaker's stand where John Kidder of Kentucky made beaver hats for the swells at $12 apiece. Two hand-operated fire engines were placed in a Spritzhaus and a volunteer fire brigade was formed. The construction of the main line of the Grand Trunk Railway through the village brought promise of greatness and some Irish laborers. Lots on King Street sold for $250. A Mechanics Institute was opened and people could exchange library books every Saturday night. A £300 contract was awarded to Jacob Y. Shantz to lay wooden sidewalks on one side of the central streets – King, Queen, Frederick, Benton and Weber.

Waterloo was not doing so well: it had only 250 people. Jacob Snider, who had bought Abe Erb's pioneer holdings, owned most of the land along one side of King Street and wanted to keep it for his children. Not until 1854 did the enterprising John Hoffman and Isaac Weber persuade him to sell his precious acres. They were surveyed and staked off into building lots. The new owners didn't wait for tardy settlers to come and buy: they advertised a picnic. A large wagon drawn by an ox team was loaded with refreshments – liquid and solid; an auctioneer took his stand in the middle and was moved from lot to lot while a crowd of people followed, eating, drinking, and bidding, till all the drinks were gone and all the land was sold.

Waterloo's population was doubled within a year. Factories began to rise out of the swampland. They made buggies, boots, and chairs; one shop (later to become The Waterloo Manufacturing Company) engaged sixteen hands and an eight-horse-power engine to make mechanical threshing equipment. The grist mill was more than an industry: it gave sociability and overnight shelter to pioneer farmers who travelled two or three days over rough trails to reach the settlement with their grain. A monthly livestock market, where citizens came to buy pigs to fatten in their own back yards, made the corner of King and William Streets the liveliest place in the hamlet. P. E. W. Moyer, publishing *The Waterloo Chronicle*, the community's first English newspaper, told all about it.

Waterloo was incorporated as a village in 1857. Jacob Snider donated a site for a municipal building and the village council chose a beehive as a device for a corporate seal that would symbolize the busy community.

Joseph Seagram came to Waterloo in 1857 and bought the grist mill whose side line was Alte Korn-schnapps (Old Rye Whisky). When distilling became the most profitable operation and he could afford to build a mansion, Joe Seagram bought the Greenbush between the two villages where young Berliners and Waterlooers used to waylay each other and battle with bare-fists. When the land was surveyed it was discovered that it lay entirely in Berlin! Joseph Seagram was so loyal to Waterloo that he wouldn't live in the rival village: he gave the land away – as a site for a hospital that would serve both communities.

Berlin continued to prosper. Small factories sprang up like weeds. Reinhold Lang started a tan-

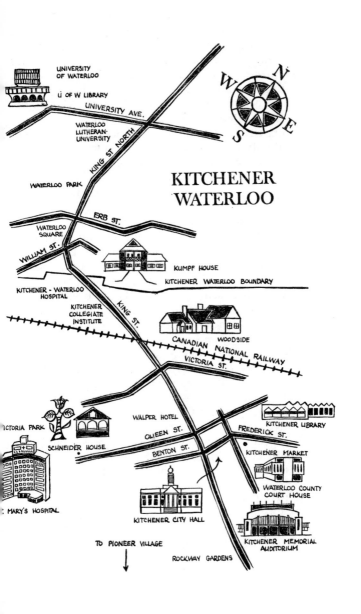

nery with his sons sweating over the vats. John Woelfle began making plows. Peter Hymmen opened a tinsmithing shop. Carl von Ahrens, a nobleman's son, made stoves and machines. John Motz and Fred Rittinger established the German *Berliner Journal* (which became the *Kitchener-Waterloo Record*).

Louis Breithaupt came to Berlin to buy hides; he married and founded a tannery. His wife kept the family by boarding the tannery workmen so all the profits could be turned back into the business. They built a large brick house with a tower, drove in a carriage and were highly respected. They had faith in Berlin: they bought property and in 1862 built the American Hotel for $9000.

The Breithaups worked hard for the community and the country. So did their sons and grandsons: they were always in public office. Three Louis Breithaupts have been mayors, two have been members of Parliament, and when Louis Breithaupt III was appointed Ontario's Lieutenant-Governor one local woman expressed the opinion of many: "I'm glad they put Louis in," she said, "he's not stuck up, he's not a boozer, and he sure is nice-looking."

The 1860's saw many advancements. Berlin got its first sewer. Females wishing to study French and higher mathematics were admitted to the grammar school. St. Jerome's College was founded. Sportsmen hunted wild turkeys – the wolves and bears having disappeared. The House of Refuge was established. Mount Hope Cemetery was started. Waterloo's population had again doubled – to 1273: half were native Canadians, 450 came from the German States and Holland, 65 from the British Isles.

The first of Waterloo's insurance companies, The Waterloo Mutual Fire and The Mutual Life of Canada, were begun in the 1860's by solid local citizens who went to other solid local citizens and said, "If you got a little money you'd like to put in we think we could start a company; we don't promise big returns but if we get into this thing together we might make ourselves a little bit." The North Waterloo Farmers Mutual Fire, the Economical Mutual Fire (in Berlin), and the Dominion Life were begun soon after and in the same way. (The Equitable Life and Canada Health and Accident came later.) The combined companies now engage over 1500 local employees, have agents all over Canada, and assets that affect the economy of the nation. They are still managed by solid local citizens.

Berlin became a town with 3000 people in 1870. Dr. William Pipe, six feet, six inches tall, was the first mayor. Blocks of stores were solid on King Street and there were fourteen churches. A constable was appointed. On nights when there was no moonlight several coal-oil lamps were lit at downtown intersections. Peter X. Moyer printed the town's first daily paper. Jacob Kaufman started a planing mill. George Debus, the dapper barber, trimmed beards, expounded on politics, and every Friday pulled teeth.

A Board of Trade was organized in Berlin as more one-man shops grew into factories. As furniture-makers Krug, Baetz, Hibner and Anthes employed more and more men, they called Berlin The Furniture Capital of Canada. George Rumpel came to Berlin to sing in a saengerfest and stayed to become The Felt Shoe King of Canada. J. M. Schneider who worked in a button factory for $1 a day, began making sausages at night in the basement of his cottage home, starting an industry that has earned Kitchener the title of Canada's Sausage City.

A governor-general visited the area and on seeing

street after street of substantial brick houses, asked where the working men lived. Most of the people in both towns owned their own homes. The newcomer who wanted to belong couldn't live in a rented house or run up a grocery bill. There was no tolerance for the four-flusher, for anyone who could afford only cotton but was wearing silk. When a stranger came to town people asked, "What's he got?" If the answer was, "He hasn't got much but he's a worker and a saver," they'd say, "Then he's all right." Hard-headed citizens applauded the man who built himself a cellar and lived in it until he had saved enough money to add a main floor: that was the kind of solidity they believed in.

The majority didn't care much for higher education. Boys and girls left school early, worked in a factory or clerked in a store and gave their earnings to mama. In the evenings they helped with the baking and mending or worked in the garden or woodshed with papa; on Thursday nights they went to a band concert, on Friday to choir practice, on Sunday they attended church and strolled on the boardwalk between the two towns. The children of the town's High Society attended boarding schools in Galt and Toronto.

Waterloo built a town hall for $10,000 in 1874 and boasted thirteen taverns, an Orpheus and Harmony Hall where every other night the members would gather to sing and draw beer from a barrel. But they went home early to their comfortable wives and got up at five to work. Every Sunday after church they took their round-cheeked families and their picnic baskets filled with braunschweiger, "bretzels" and pilsener to the park or a grove on Buck's Hill where the singing master led them in a joyful saengerei.

84

The two towns grew closer together. The board-walk that joined them was a favourite promenade; a horsecar ran back and forth, clanging a cowbell at midnight to warn lingering swains to catch the last ride or walk home. Jointly the two towns built a grammar school on the site of the present Kitchener Collegiate; they attended each other's balls and joined one another's Vereine (societies). The Schuetzenverein (shooting club) had an underground gallery, its members wore Tyrolese dress and prac-tised hitting a target. The Turnverein exercised on poles, swings and racks; they arranged numerous social gatherings and paraded in white cloaks and caps. The Gesangvereine (singing societies) sang cantatas and held international Saengerfests; cedar arches decorated the streets, bands and choirs came from far-away cities, and thousands of people in costume paraded to the park where they gorged on frankfurters, lager, and Strauss.

The population of Berlin and Waterloo almost doubled during the 80's and cows were no longer allowed to roam the streets. Mennonites from the country came to work in the towns; more Germans and British moved in. MacMahons, Evans, and Jacksons married Schnitzlers, Lingelbachs, and Ebys; Englishmen ate sauerkraut and Germans learned to play bagpipes. In Berlin's park they erected a more-than-life-size statue of a rotund Queen Victoria and a bust of Kaiser Wilhelm I wearing a spiked military helmet and old English muttonchops.

John King, Q.C., married to the daughter of rebel William Lyon Mackenzie, displayed in the parlor of their Benton Street home an 1837 poster offering a large reward for the capture of Mrs. King's father alive or dead. The poster was hidden away when they moved to "Woodside", a more pretentious house which is now preserved as a national shrine to honour their son Billy.

There had been a tavern on the southwest corner of King and Queen streets in Berlin since 1835. In 1892 Abel Walper bought the site for a large red-brick hotel. Before he began building he offered to sell to the town for $500 a strip of land that would straighten the jog at the intersection. The council accepted his offer but there was so much criticism of their extravagance that they let it drop.

At the beginning of the new century Berlin, with almost 10,000 people, was bristling with culture. The Ladies' Emerson Club made systematic studies of the best English literature. In the Opera House behind the Walper Hotel the Berlin Dramatic Society presented Faust and Uncle Tom's Cabin. The Frauenvereine (women's societies) of the churches held soirées. The W.C.T.U. erected an ornamental fountain in Berlin's civic square. The Berlin Public Library was built by the Carnegie Foundation.

Waterloo boasted an interest in the Sport of Kings. When the Seagram Stable made itself known as the greatest in North America, the town adopted as its official colors the stable's victorious yellow and black.

In January 1900 George Schlee came down town wearing the first pair of rubbers made in Berlin. Soon after, Jacob Kaufman organized the Merchants Rubber, John Forsyth started making shirts, A. B. Pollock and Alec Welker manufactured a gramaphone that led to Dominion Electrohome Industries.

At a Board of Trade banquet in 1902, E. W. B. Snider, M.P.P. for Waterloo North, suggested that Berlin, Waterloo, and other nearby towns might unite in getting electric power from Niagara Falls. Dan B. Detweiler of Berlin was so excited by the idea that he was appointed a committee of one to implement the proposal. On his bicycle and at his own expense he rode from town to town to persuade officials and manufacturers to attend a conference in Berlin. As an outcome of the meeting a deputation of 1500 people went to Toronto to petition the government to act. The Hon. Adam Beck introduced a bill in the legislature which resulted in the foundation of the Ontario Hydro Electric Power Commission.

On October 11, 1910, Berlin was the first distant municipality to be flooded with light from Niagara. The town celebrated for three days.

Berlin aspired to triple its population in five years. It went after outside industries, offering to pay their moving expenses, give them free factory sites, and the most skilful, conscientious workmen in the country. In a year eight new firms started, fourteen existing ones built large additions, and the Dominion Rubber Company contracted to erect a tire factory that would employ 2000 people.

As the twelfth stroke of Berlin's post-office clock died away at midnight on June 10, 1912, Berlin's portly Mayor, William Schmalz, stepped out on a platform at the town hall, twisted the waxed tips of his moustache, and proclaimed that Busy Berlin was a City. Six thousand people in the square cheered and embraced one another, the band played, church bells rang, giant firecrackers exploded, rejoicing citizens danced up and down King Street till roosters in the back yards started to crow.

The new city prospered. MADE IN BERLIN labels went all over Canada on a hundred different products. A city planning committee started preparing for a population of 50,000 people.

Then came war with Germany the Fatherland.

Gentle old Professor Wiegand, who wore a little

shoulder cape, lost his job teaching German in the public schools. Children paraded with Union Jacks and sold tags to raise money for the Red Cross. Young men enlisted in the 118th Battalion and were billeted on straw ticks in Rumpel's felt factory. The bust of Kaiser Wilhelm was toppled from its pedestal in Victoria Park and dumped in the weedy waters of the lake. Women went to the churches and prayed that the war would be over before anyone was hurt.

Several Berlin boys were killed in France. Feeling against Germany ran high.

There were nasty rumours that the bust of the old Kaiser, rescued from the lake, was hidden in the hall of the Concordia Club (a Gesangverein founded in 1873). One night fifty soldiers stormed up the stairs to the Concordia Hall and found the bust in a closet. They ripped pictures from the walls, smashed dishes, tossed a piano, chairs and tables through the second storey windows into King Street and burned them in a giant bonfire. Singing "We'll Never Let the Old Flag Fall," they triumphantly carried the 150-pound bust of Old Bill to their barracks, wrapped it in potato sacking and hid it in the guard-house.

Meanwhile Berlin manufacturers got letters from customers all over the country saying they couldn't sell goods with Made in Berlin labels and their accounts would be withdrawn if the city didn't get rid of the name of the Kaiser's evil nest. Canadian newspapers called Berlin pro-German.

The accusation stung. Citizens of pioneer blood were hurt and bewildered: they had been born in Canada, some were of the fourth generation, all their dreaming and striving were for Busy Berlin and Canada, first, last, and always. Many agreed that Berlin's name would have to be changed if its manufacturers were to stay in business. Others loved the name and stubbornly determined to keep it; they formed a Citizen's League and started a vigorous campaign.

The name changers formed the British League to oppose them. The two daily newspapers took sides. Mass meetings were held. Friends and neighbours quarrelled. Families were divided. Arguments fanned into fracas. Several leading citizens were given a cold and undignified dunking in the shallow water of Victoria Park's mud-bottomed lake. The local M.P.P. was marched down the street by soldiers and forced to kiss the flag on the steps of the city hall. One newspaper office was smashed – but on the same day the enterprising publisher was able to bring out an extra edition telling all about it.

A plebiscite was drawn up to find out the will of the people: 1569 voted in favour of changing the name; 1488 opposed it and as many others stayed home and didn't vote at all.

The new name was selected from thousands submitted in a city-sponsored contest. Kitchener was chosen because it was currently in the news, the Irish war lord having recently gone to his death.

On September 1, 1916, Berlin, Ontario, Canada, ceased to exist.

Kitchener was a different city: girls no longer had to be able to speak German to get jobs in its stores; no German was preached in its churches; all its people spoke English: "Look once the window out," they'd cry, "the street comes marching down with soldiers." A thousand K-W boys – half of them with German names – crossed the sea to fight against Germany.

Waterloo had the distinction of subscribing more money for Victory Bonds in proportion to its population than any other town in Canada.

When peace was restored Kitchener and Waterloo thought again of expansion. An energetic Chamber of Commerce enticed American industries to locate in Kitchener. It became the greatest rubber manufacturer in the British Empire. Immigrant workers from all over Europe moved in, giving the community a cosmopolitan air – and an onion-domed church.

Mabel Dunham, Kitchener's librarian, wrote *The Trail of the Conestoga*, a story of the Mennonite pioneers that filled all their descendants with pride. Isaiah Bowman, of Waterloo Mennonite stock, was president of Johns Hopkins University. Orie Walper, whose father built the hotel, invented plaster lath. K-W schools were educating Walter Zinn, now one of America's atomic scientists, journalists Biland Honderich, June Calwood, David Spurgeon and Kenneth and Margaret Sturm Millar who write crime novels in California.

World War II found the Twin Cities eager to beat the Nazis. When Canada was about to disband her only tank regiment, Kitchener and Waterloo organized a Buy-a-Tank drive which was waged with such vigor and publicity that within a week twice the objective was raised and the Canadian Government was convinced that Canada must have an armored corps.

K-W war production was colossal; its war service record was unsurpassed in the country.

Forty-five hundred K-W men and women came home after the war. They were followed by thousands of immigrants – mostly from Germany – and by many Canadians who wanted a good place to live. A fringe of new houses grew around the adjoining communities. Crosstown buses shuttled in every direction; lumbering old street cars were replaced by the first trolley coaches to be operated in Ontario.

Waterloo-Wellington Airport was developed to serve the two counties.

Waterloo, with only slightly over 10,000 people, decided that though a population of 15,000 was required for incorporation as a city, the town was so mature, so outstanding in industry, finance and prestige that it should be granted unusual consideration. A town committee persuaded the Ontario legislature to pass a special act of parliament and on January 1, 1948, Waterloo became a city – and celebrated with a carnival in its new Memorial Arena.

Both cities were busy as beavers. Europeans were being taught to speak English, Canadian newcomers were learning how to make shnitz pie and sour cream salads. There were picnics, band concerts and celebrations in the parks. Every night there were bingo games and bowling, choir and orchestra practice, concerts and amateur plays. There were so many clubs and organizations that almost every citizen was president or treasurer of something. Fifty-six churches serving twenty-seven denominations, with Roman Catholics and Lutherans leading, made it as hard to find car-parking space on a Sunday as it was on a weekday.

Nothing but the best was good enough for the happily married cities. Their penny-pinching economy gave them millions to spend – on essentials. Modern elementary schools were built. Kitchener's new incinerator was the last word in disposal. The K-W Hospital added a nine-storey $3,000,000 building that was so far ahead of the times that delegations came from the u.s. and all over Canada to study its services. Carl Rieder, a local architect, made plans for several collegiates, Kitchener's police building, and a public library.

Sports fans who wanted to see Kitchener turn out

more hockey stars like the famous Kraut line formed a committee that persuaded the ratepayers to pass a bylaw providing $450,000 for a memorial auditorium. Building prices sky-rocketed but Kitchener got its arena just the same – at a cost of one and a quarter million. And citizens proudly thought it was worth it when the K-W Dutchmen twice won Canada's senior hockey championship and represented the nation at the Olympics.

In 1954 Kitchener's 52,733 people celebrated the centenary of its incorporation. There was a gigantic parade, a revue of the century, a Hofbrau where they served pigs' tails and sauerkraut. For a week people danced on the street every night and bought wooden nickels as souvenirs. Kitchener's growth was declared to be like the sweeping surge of a tide. The city doubled its area by annexing 3,500 acres. The planning commission was preparing for a population of 100,000.

In the next fifteen years Kitchener's population almost doubled. On a per capita basis, Kitchener and Waterloo were the fastest growing cities in Ontario – after metro Toronto. Thousands of new houses were built throughout the communities and in subdivisions surrounding them. Apartment buildings kept rising. New office buildings and stores kept appearing. Little shops sprang up everywhere. Old factories put on additions and many huge new ones were built.

K-W natives said, "The towns don't look like they used to." Elms and maples that once shaded their grandmothers were being cut down to widen the streets. Shopping plazas appeared in residential areas. Red-brick Victorian mansions were removed to make room for new buildings. Behind King Street, houses, shops and Kitchener's old red fire hall were levelled to provide civic parking lots.

The Twin Cities began to look modern. The Waterloo Trust and Savings Company built the first sky-scraper – 12 storeys high. Kitchener's imposing new police building was erected with a blue vitrolite front. Waterloo tore down the old soot-gray factories that defaced one side of its main business area and developed Waterloo Square with a tall building to house municipal offices and a shopping mall surrounded by a paved lot where cars could be parked free of charge. A 10-storey addition made St. Mary's a General Hospital. The new Public Library in Kitchener was acclaimed the most beautiful building in western Ontario. The charming 100-year-old County Court House was scrapped and replaced by a handsome concrete edifice with a beak-like canopy that suggests the covering of a Conestoga wagon.

The most revolutionary change in the community has been taking place in Waterloo with the miraculous development of two universities: Waterloo Luthern University and the University of Waterloo. Growing explosively, they have become the city's greatest "industry", have greatly boosted its population and prestige, have given new cultural dimension with public lectures, drama festivals, concerts, art exhibits, and student activities that shock a staid populace. The scientific research facilities of the University of Waterloo, including a computer centre and department of design, are an invaluable resource for local industry.

The universities started when Waterloo's Lutheran Seminary, founded in 1911, offered arts courses to non-theological students and evolved Waterloo College, affiliated with the University of Western

Ontario. In 1953, J. Gerald Hagey, a graduate and a member of the college board, gave up his position as advertising manager of Canadian Goodrich to become president of his little alma mater. He suggested the addition of an associate faculty in science and a co-operative school of engineering in which students would alternately spend four months at school and four months in practical employment during their five-year university education.

To receive necessary provincial support, a completely new, non-denominational institution, the University of Waterloo, was launched – with the assistance of members of the local community. A 1000 acre campus was purchased in 1958 and building was begun. Several churches affiliated with the new university and started to build residential colleges: St. Jerome's (Roman Catholic), Renison (Anglican), Conrad Grebel (Mennonite), and St. Paul's (United).

In 1960 the Lutherans, with three buildings already established on their own campus, decided to remain autonomous as Waterloo Lutheran University, to develop their own programme in arts, science, business administration, and graduate schools in theology and social work. Limiting enrolment to 2400, they are aiming for a friendly community of learning housed on their 45 acre campus where there are now sixteen buildings with more being planned.

The University of Waterloo in the twelve years since its inception has become the third major university in the province – after Toronto and Western. It has vast modern buildings for instruction in engineering, mathematics, science, arts, physical education and graduate studies, a spectacular seven-storey library, a theatre, and a stadium

– donated by Seagram's; a student village, four church college residences and a co-op student apartment building house forty per cent of its more than 9000 students.

The University of Waterloo has Canada's largest engineering college. Its co-op system, unique in Canada, has been extended to mathematics, physics, chemistry, physical education, psychology, architecture, as well as engineering. The university's rapid growth rate, research opportunities, year-round employment and outstanding graduate school have attracted top professors and students from all round the world.

Because of the fantastic plans, growth, and rapid changes being made in Kitchener and Waterloo, figures quoted today might be obsolete in a month – or tomorrow. People keep moving in: there are almost as many enterprising newcomers as there are energetic natives. New buildings seem to pop up overnight, high-rise apartments are becoming commonplace, shopping malls rival the finest in Canada. Both cities have expropriated property and begun to build vast civic centres. Farms within the communities' ever-extending borders are bulldozed and levelled for housing subdivisions and industrial parks. Great sprawling factories keep gobbling up municipal sites as fast as the cities can prepare them. Rows of old buildings are demolished to make way for streets that divert traffic from the crowded hearts of the cities, ring roads and expressways are in constant construction.

Kitchener is beginning to look big, to think big, to be a big city – while Waterloo independently grows along with it. Together they have almost 400 miles of streets, 60 schools, 107 churches, 7 golf courses. K-W industrial lists total more than 1500 company names with 400 factories sending diversified products all around the world.

Kitchener-Waterloo's joint population is almost 140,000; town planners are talking about a metro area that will have half a million people within twenty-five years. All of Waterloo Township, they say, will soon become urban. Waterloo's function in the regional pattern will be largely residential and academic. Kitchener by the year 2000 will have reached skyward, with its downtown core transformed to a sunny pedestrian mall where people can shop, socialize, admire fountains and flowers, be entertained, and do business.

In the meantime the Walper Hotel still obstructs traffic at Kitchener's busiest intersection – and serves the best sauerkraut and haute cuisine in western Ontario. Trumpet bands still parade through Waterloo and put on tattoos with fireworks in the park. The Concordia is still the largest social club in the Twin Cities. Hard-headed K-W citizens still work in their shirt sleeves and applaud employees who buy a home and save their money. Their wives still fanatically clean their houses, crochet lace doilies and prefer a cooking school to a fashion show. And every Saturday morning they all crowd into the old red market building behind the city hall where farm women wearing the bonnets and plain clothes of the various Mennonite sects, come – as they have done for a hundred and thirty years – to sell tiny cobs of pickled corn, apple butter, schwadamahga sausage, and black velvet cushion tops with doves and "love" and "Grandmother" worked on them in tufted colored wool.